SPACESHIPS AND POLITICS

D1603659

SPACESHIPS AND POLITICS
The Political Theory of Rod Serling

Leslie Dale Feldman

LEXINGTON BOOKS
A division of
ROWMAN & LITTLEFIELD PUBLISHERS, INC.
Lanham • Boulder • New York • Toronto • Plymouth, UK

Published by Lexington Books
A division of Rowman & Littlefield Publishers, Inc.
A wholly owned subsidiary of The Rowman & Littlefield Publishing Group, Inc.
4501 Forbes Boulevard, Suite 200, Lanham, Maryland 20706
http://www.lexingtonbooks.com

Estover Road, Plymouth PL6 7PY, United Kingdom

British Library Cataloguing in Publication Information Available

Library of Congress Cataloging-in-Publication Data

Feldman, Leslie Dale.
  Spaceships and politics : the political theory of Rod Serling / Leslie Dale
Feldman.
    p. cm.
  Includes bibliographical references and index.
  ISBN 978-0-7391-2044-6 (cloth : alk. paper) — ISBN 978-0-7391-2045-3 (pbk. : alk.
paper) — ISBN 978-0-7391-5051-1 (electronic)
  1. Twilight zone (Television program : 1959-1964) 2. Serling, Rod, 1924-1975—
Criticism and interpretation. I. Title.
  PN1992.77.T87F45 2010
  791.45'72--dc22

                                                                    2010022527

Printed in the United States of America

To My Parents

Contents

Preface

How do we think about human nature, the individual and the state, dictatorship and democracy? What is the individual's place in the political order?

For Rod Serling all of these things were part of how we think about life on this planet. In *The Twilight Zone*, Serling considers all aspects of human nature and politics, often a reflection of the politics of the time—the Cold War, conformity, nuclear war and post-industrial technological society—in the setting of aliens and other planets but the messages are political.

Serling was a student of human nature using fantasy and the supernatural to illustrate political ideas. As JFK said in a 1963 speech at American University, discussing the U.S. and the USSR, "we all inhabit this small planet," and, for Serling, that planet is the vehicle to study our place in the universe and the role of the individual and the state.

Rod Serling was perhaps television's most brilliant writer and his work includes a vast compendium of creative dramas and teleplays. This book will consider the work for which he is most famous, his masterpiece of creative thinking, *The Twilight Zone*, and the political themes for which it is famous, using mainly those shows written by Rod Serling.

Acknowledgments

I WOULD LIKE TO THANK HOFSTRA UNIVERSITY for granting me a sabbatical to complete this work. Thanks to President Stuart Rabinowitz, Provost Herman Berliner, Dean Bernard Firestone of Hofstra College of Liberal Arts, Prof. Emeritus Mark Landis and Rosanna Perotti, Chair of the Political Science department for providing research resources and time with which to use them. Michelle Wu of Hofstra Law School provided valuable advice, as did Rob Tempio of Princeton University Press. Mark Labaton provided advice and support which is greatly appreciated.

I wish to thank the many faculty members who have encouraged me, including Werner Dannhauser, Isaac Kramnick, Jeremy Rabkin and Woody Kelley of Cornell, Alan Ryan of Oxford and Princeton, and Bertell Ollman and H. Mark Roelofs of New York University. Bertell Ollman's book *Alienation* was particularly useful for this study. Special thanks to David Theodosopoulos and Roni Mueller at CBS for their kind consideration. The work could not have come to fruition without their help and it is greatly appreciated. Thanks also to Joseph Parry, Erin Walpole, Alden Perkins, and Paula Durbin-Westby of Lexington Books. Two resources that were also invaluable are Marc Scott Zicree's *Twilight Zone Companion* and Gordon Sander's *Serling: The Rise and Twilight of Television's Last Angry Man.* The Paley Center in Los Angeles was a superb resource and a treasure trove for research. Thanks also to Lawrence M. Krauss and Noel Carroll and Jodi Dean, Robert Lincoln, Steve Satz, Yvette Marqueen, and Maria at the LA County Library in Santa Monica.

My friends at the post office, Gene, Mary, Sung and Kevin, were congenial and supportive, which I appreciated. Many thanks to Gene Martone for the Rod Serling stamps.

Thanks to Eunemone and Simona Fordyce for identifying "Spring Song" in "Miniature," "Romeo and Juliet Overture" in "The Chaser," "The Anvil Chorus" in "Once Upon a Time," and "The Emperor Waltz" in "The After Hours." In addition, Peter Molesso was an early inspiration who encouraged me to write this work, Bob Hymes escorted me to the Paley Center in Los Angeles, Mary Starke was a source of support, as were Ginny Greenberg, Miguel Pozo, Chris Vaccaro, Sheryl Perry, Wigberto Serpa, Maria Figueroa, Kaytee Lozier, a fellow *Twilight Zone* fan, Martine and Bongo, Dukie, and Tuffy and Lola.

Robert Greenberg, Esq., has been a generous source of support and encouragement, humor and advice for which I am very grateful. He helped this work come to fruition with his guidance, enthusiasm and friendship. He has been a wonderful and loyal friend and it is only with his encouragement that I was able to persevere.

I wish to thank my parents, Simon and Phoebe Feldman, for their love and support. Their advice has been the hedge that has kept me in my way. This book would not have been written without their constant support, patience, finely-honed editorial, negotiating and managerial skills, and selfless devotion, a gift I could not have asked for but am grateful to have received. Words cannot express my profound thanks, gratitude, appreciation, admiration and love.

I wish to thank Dr. Clifford Feldman and Dr. Tina Verder for their tremendous effort on behalf of this work which could not have been completed without them. The time and energy they put into seeing this work completed is greatly appreciated, as is their undaunted work, time and energy on my behalf. Jacob and Sam Feldman were similarly supportive and enthusiastic about the work, especially when we watched the marathons and on the (miniature) golf course. Ditto S and K.

Susan Kleinman has been a great source of support and encouragement without which this work could not have been completed. Her thoughts and suggestions helped provide needed inspiration and she was an enthusiastic research assistant who rescued me—thanks for being my parachute. Thanks also to Bradley and Stefanie Kleinman for their enthusiastic support.

Thanks to Sir Bongo Igitur (commonly known as "Iggy") Wickersham whose undying efforts to worm his way methodically through mountains of literature helped me establish the roots of this opus.

Finally, thanks to Rod Serling for continuing to make us think about our politics and our planet.

Introduction

R OD SERLING WAS RANKED #1 IN *TV Guide*'s list of the 25 Greatest Sci-Fi Legends.[1] But his writing was more than science fiction, it was also political theory. When asked about the Iranian president's visit to the United Nations, former ambassador John Bolton said, "You should treat this as an off Broadway production," and he described the UN as a "Twilight Zone."[2] Ambassador Bolton was on to something. When I was in graduate school friends would never let me watch *The Twilight Zone*. *The Twilight Zone* was my favorite television show and I had to sneak to watch it. I couldn't figure out why, but they simply did not approve. "It's scary" they said. Rod Serling's vision of humanity—for that is what he portrays in *The Twilight Zone*, even as he uses aliens and beings from other worlds to do it—has a nasty edge to it. The edge, and the nasty glimpse of humanity, have decided Hobbesian qualities. Though Serling was writing worlds away in time and place from Thomas Hobbes (who wrote in seventeenth century England) he managed to infuse *The Twilight Zone* with much of Hobbesian "nastiness." According to *Webster's* twilight refers to "a state of imperfect clarity, of dubiety, indefiniteness or indistinctness, of . . . darkness or gloom."

Examples of the nastiness and depressing and violent nature of humans abound in such episodes as "To Serve Man," "Time Enough at Last," "The Monsters are due on Maple Street," "People Are Alike All Over," "The Shelter," etc. which are infused with a vision of humanity that, to Hobbes, was "solitary, poore, nasty, brutish . . ." and to Serling if not poor then solitary, nasty and brutish. Many of Serling's visions are violent and he is often preoccupied with nuclear holocaust which is featured in several shows such as "The Shelter" and

"Time Enough at Last." Included in the catalogue of violence is a man getting run over by a car ("What You Need") a man running a boy over with a car ("You Drive") several shows where people jump or are thrown out of windows ("Perchance to Dream," "The Fever," "A Most Unusual Camera," "What's In the Box?") and one where a man commits suicide by jumping from a train ("A Stop at Willoughby").

There are executions, a man who is chased into a pool by his machines ("The Trouble with Machines"), a man who is paralyzed by the devil ("The Howling Man"), a man who murders his fellow bank robber ("Rip Van Winkle Caper"), a man who slits his own throat ("The Silence"), a man who is pinned to a grave, a man whose head is cut off and put on a jack in the box ("It's a Good Life"), a man who is dinner for a hungry alien ("To Serve Man"), a man who is shot by a Mexican police officer even though he has a cure for cancer ("The Gift"), a man who shoots his daughter's boyfriend after he sells him his compassion ("The Self Improvement of Salvadore Ross"), a fading movie star who stays young by turning journalists to dust ("Queen of the Nile"), a ventriloquist who is turned into a puppet by his dummy ("The Dummy"), a man who pushes his wife off the roof ("Escape Clause"), and a man who is killed by a doll ("Living Doll").

Why, according to Serling, is violence and nastiness the thematic thread that connects both aliens and Earth dwellers and that characterizes the human (and alien) condition? To understand this we must understand the importance of the concept of fear and how it is used in *The Twilight Zone*. The concept of fear is an important political concept dating from the origin of power. As Machiavelli famously said "it is better to be feared than loved." The political philosopher who, perhaps more than anyone else, understood the importance of fear to power and politics and in human relations was Thomas Hobbes.

For Hobbes, humans are motivated by "diffidence" or fear—fear of each other primarily that drives them to form societies and governments for the purpose of protection. Fear is a great human motivator and protection a great need. But more than this, humans are acquisitive and belligerent. They are violent and self-serving. Serling agreed.

Serling clearly had something of the Hobbesian dark side to his personality. On a Dick Cavett show in response to the host mentioning a *TV Guide* article on Serling which described him as depressed Serling replied "I read it and didn't realize it was about me. . . . I'm not depressed" and then jokes "I'm hanging myself on a lamppost right after the show."[3] Clearly Serling had a fascination with politics, in the same show remarking to a news reporter "you now qualify as a science fiction personality, you've been to a political convention and that's about as bizarre as you can get."

Serling's negative worldview is clearly expressed in *The Twilight Zone*. Those who are treated inhumanely treat others inhumanely—and even those who are treated humanely treat others inhumanely ("It's a Good Life" comes to mind) This twilight landscape of gray to black can be seen in a variety of episodes including "The Eye of the Beholder," "A Most Unusual Camera," "Dust," "The Rip Van Winkle Caper," "To Serve Man," and many others. Humans are seen as frightened, subject to the fear instilled by the state and by other people, as well as self interested, greedy and willing to believe the worst about others. These character traits are often reflected in the aliens that populate *The Twilight Zone*.

Serling takes up other themes of Hobbes, notably the modern capitalist "rat race" the race for social mobility or "race of life." In these episodes (including "The Bewitchin' Pool," "A Stop at Willoughby," "Uncle Simon," "The Masks") the race for social mobility is seen as shallow and often destructive. Social mobility and wealth are achieved at the price of peace of mind, peace and quiet, values and decency. Frequently in these episodes Serling shows glimpses of happy simpler days that hark back to the nineteenth century before society became so competitive, shallow and materialistic. In at least one episode ("The Bewitchin' Pool") a swimming pool is used as the Hollywood symbol of glittery shallowness (note: this episode, written by Earl Hamner, Jr., incorporates his themes very well).

Like Hobbes, Serling has a mechanistic view of the world. Often he pictures man as machine or, as Hobbes said, "automata" which for Hobbes was "but a motion of limbs." Additionally, Serling pictures man struggling with machines or men and women as robots. These episodes include "I Sing the Body Electric"—where a family hires a robot nanny, "Steel"—where boxers are robots, "Uncle Simon"—where a rich man becomes a robot, "The Lonely"—where a man who is banished to another planet has a robot girlfriend, "The Mighty Casey"—where a baseball player is a robot, "The Lateness of the Hour"—where a daughter is a robot, "From Agnes with Love"—where a computer falls in love with a man, "A Thing about Machines"—where a man is hounded by machines and run over by a car that drives itself, "The After Hours"—where mannequins are people, and "The Brain Center at Whipple's" where a manager is replaced by a robot who has his mannerisms.

Serling's *Twilight Zone* expresses the frustrations with modern life and particularly the monotony and conformity of mass culture which play on man's aggressive and belligerent nature. In themes that are reminiscent of De Tocqueville Serling denounces conformity of thought, word and dress, the need to look and think alike that accompanies contemporary bourgeois society. In a very famous *Twilight Zone* episode, "The Eye of the Beholder," shadowy figures in a hospital take care of a patient whose head is swathed in bandages. She has had plastic surgery to improve her appearance because it is unacceptable. But when the bandages are taken off, and the doctor drops his knife for dramatic effect, we see that she is beautiful and the doctors and nurses are deformed. The point is that the patient (Donna Douglas from *The Beverly Hillbillies*) doesn't conform in a society (like our own?) that prizes conformity. To reinforce this theme a dictator is shown on state television promoting the value of "one idea, one truth, one ideology" and presumably one appearance.

"Lookism" and "ageism" are considered, usually in the context of a fascist communal state where everyone must look alike and individualism is not rewarded. "Eye of the Beholder" is the most famous of these episodes, but it is also considered in "Mr. Bevis," "A Short Drink From a Certain Fountain" and "The Trade Ins." Such episodes as "Eye of the Beholder," "The Obsolete Man," "It's a Good Life," "Number Twelve Looks Just Like You" emphasize the dissatisfaction with mass culture and modern, bourgeois conformity—of thought, word, deed and looks—that was becoming part of life as Serling knew it. In "Number Twelve Looks Just Like You" Serling envisions a world in which everyone is compelled to have plastic surgery to look good. When you reach a certain age you must pick out the model that you want to look like from a catalogue which, presumably, is set up by the state. Hobbes said "Nature hath made men so equal" but here the state comes in to equalize them—even in terms of looks.

Perhaps this critique of conformity was Serling's way of indicating that, though he moved to Hollywood, he hadn't sold out his values of decency and social commitment. "Be Ashamed to die until you have won some victory for humanity." The Horace Mann quote was the motto of Antioch College, Serling's alma mater, and was featured in a *Twilight Zone* episode called "The Changing of the Guard" in which Ellis Fowler, an elderly teacher at a school for boys, believes his efforts have not amounted to anything.[4] Did Serling see himself as Ellis Fowler? What was Serling's victory for mankind? Perhaps this was a concern for him considering the Antioch College mission of social activism and liberal values. *The Twilight Zone* was a safe way for Serling to communicate social and political messages while flying under the radar of the censors and remaining superficially uncontroversial. Science fiction was the perfect venue as it could hardly be considered controversial.

The social and political themes in *The Twilight Zone* include: fascism, racism, capital punishment, ageism, lookism, the individual against the state, tyranny, dictatorship. Just as professor Ellis Fowler won a victory for mankind by teaching students values that helped them win a war, perhaps Rod Serling thought he had won a victory for mankind by portraying his political ideas—the triumph of the individual, opposition to competition and capital punishment in the guise of popular culture and science fiction.

For Hobbes, humans were motivated by "diffidence" or fear. Fear has been seen during many times in American history including fear of anarchists, "the red scare," and the war on terror. Serling recognized that governments can harness this fear and deploy it to increase the power of the state. *Twilight Zone* episodes including "The Fear," "The Monsters Are Due on Maple St." and "The Shelter" play on this theme of the use of fear by governments, and sometimes aliens, to enhance power.

Serling, like Hobbes, understood that humans are only civilized under the threat of compulsion because they are by nature violent and only understand the threat of violence. If the world is going to blow up and there is a breakdown in order humans revert to their natural state—belligerent, acquisitive, and violent. As Hobbes said "if any two men desire the same thing, which neverthelesse they cannot both enjoy, they become enemies and in the way to their end . . . endeavour to destroy or subdue one another . . . and from this diffidence of one another there is no way for any man to secure himself. . . ."[5]

Serling particularly dislikes discrimination and associates it with fear of others: "there are weapons that are simply thoughts, attitudes, prejudices to be found only in the minds of men. Prejudices can kill and suspicion can destroy. And a thoughtless frightened search for a scapegoat has a fallout all its own. And the pity of it is that these things cannot be confined to *The Twilight Zone.*"[6] Similarly, "It's A Good Life" explains how people tyrannize themselves through the use of fear and how violence reinforces it.[7]

The introduction of "Five Characters in Search of an Exit" says "Five improbable entities stuck together into a pit of darkness. No logic, no reason, no explanation, just a prolonged nightmare in which fear, loneliness and the unexplainable walk hand in hand. . . . " The episodes "Dust" and "The Gift" consider racism. In "Dust" a Mexican man is to be hung. In "The Gift" a visitor to a Mexican town is thought to be an alien and killed—even though he brings a "vaccine for all kinds of cancer." At the end of "The Gift" Serling's voiceover says "Madeiro, Mexico. The present. The subject: fear. The cure: a little more faith. An Rx off the shelf, in *The Twilight Zone.*" And at the end of "No Time Like the Past" Serling quotes a poet named Lathbury: "children of yesterday, heirs of tomorrow, what are you weaving? Labor and sorrow."

Fear, loneliness and isolation play powerfully into Serling's worldview. Ultimately, everyone is isolated and alone. The concept of community is a veneer—if you scratch the surface it's a fiction. In "People are Alike All Over" Serling makes the point that people or aliens on other planets need to have "outsiders" to stigmatize and feel superior to. "The Lonely" is set on another planet where a prisoner, played by Jack Warden, is sent to a modern day Siberia. He becomes so lonely that he befriends a robot in the shape of a female, and then wants to take her with him when he is "sprung." "The Changing of the Guard," "The Hitchhiker," "Time Enough at Last," all echo this theme of isolation and alienation. Yet, perhaps isolation is preferable to the violence of humans. "Elegy" is a place where there are no humans because, to quote the character Jeremy Wickwire "there can be no peace" until there are no humans. Similarly, the character in "The Mind and the Matter" voices the opinion that "people are pigs."

Serling likes to play with the theme of weak v. powerful or "big v. small" in such episodes as "The Invaders" and "The Little People." Just as beauty is a relative term, power is a relative term. You are powerful in a world of "little people"—until someone bigger than you comes along and steps on you. This theme of "big v. small" is also explored in "The Invaders" (with Agnes Moorehead) and "Stopover in a Quiet Town" in which humans are stuck in the doll house of a child from another planet.

For Serling, community in contemporary society is a false illusion. We are not a society, but a collection of individuals each pursuing its own self-interest often in competition with others for scarce resources. For Hobbes, people made up a social contract and agreed to establish a society with laws based on self interest and modern liberal democracy was not a community—but a collection of individuals who had agreed to establish a society so that each would be protected. In a society based on self interest there is no community and this theme is seen in episodes such as "The Monsters are Due on Maple Street," "The Rip Van Winkle Caper," "The Midnight Sun" where individuals compete in a "war of all v. all" scenario.

In "The Midnight Sun" Serling imagines the two extremes—heat and cold—that the Earth is either getting too close to the sun or too far away. So people will either burn up or freeze. In this chaos, in which Serling perhaps anticipates global warming, and nuclear winter, the actress Lois Nettleton is sweating and looking for scarce resources, particularly water. This is the Hobbesian nasty and brutish "state of nature" the so called "war of all against all" where individuals show their true nature. Serling frequently focuses on this theme in the context of nuclear war where either the totalitarian state or people are instilling fear.

What does Serling expect of people in these situations—fascism, totalitarianism, racism and fear? Is Serling an optimist and does he believe democracy can prevent the scenarios of *The Twilight Zone*? Is the modern mechanistic world superficial and materialistic or can it still uphold the values espoused by Horace Mann?

Fascism is considered in episodes such as "On Thursday We Leave for Home," "Deaths-Head Revisited," "It's a Good Life." These typically feature an unlikely dictator, such as Billy Mumy in "It's a Good Life" and a heroic leader in "On Thursday" who wants to lead his followers who have been stranded on another planet even after their rescue.

Billy Mumy plays a little boy who dictates to the residents of a Midwestern American town. Because they are afraid of him they dance to his tune, or don't dance as is the case. He does not allow singing and there is only one television station. When one resident protests he is turned into a jack-in-the-box and put in the cornfield. In "Four O'Clock" a man who would turn all the people he doesn't like into little people himself turns into one at four o'clock. "The Mirror" and "Deaths-Head Revisited" consider this in a more obvious political way with Nazis and communist dictators.

Racism and prejudice are also considered in "He's Alive" and "No Time Like the Past."

The individual against the state is a theme that comes up frequently and is the theme of such episodes as "The Obsolete Man," "It's a Good Life," "The Little People." This theme is also seen as individuals against aliens in "To Serve Man," "The Fear," "People Are Alike All Over." Considering many of these shows were written during the cold war the aliens could represent communists. In "The Fear" Americans stand up to an inflated alien (communists?) and "The Whole Truth" is about JFK, the Soviets and a used car salesman selling a car that makes you tell the truth.

What about democracy? Does Serling see a place for it or are humans too ruthless and competitive to participate in democracy? Are there any optimistic episodes in *The Twilight Zone*? Serling considers nuclear holocaust in at least six ("One More Pallbearer," "The Shelter," "Time Enough at Last," "Probe 7," "Two," and "Third from the Sun") episodes and optimistic episodes are not plentiful. "One for the Angels," "The Changing of the Guard," and "The Fear" can be considered optimistic. But does Serling ever consider democracy as a good system? Perhaps in "On Thursday We Leave for Home" democracy and individualism are seen as good. And, for Serling, the individual standing up to the state is good in "The Obsolete Man."

But more often modern bourgeois society is seen as promoting materialist values that do not make for better people or a good society. Images such as swimming pools, cars, money and servants, mirrors and mansions reinforce the vast emptiness of wealth and loneliness of contemporary society. Rich people are not depicted as generous but as scheming and duplicitous. Examples include "A Stop at Willoughby" (Gart's wife Janie is an example of the empty materialist), "A Thing about Machines" (Mr. Finchley is haughty), "Uncle Simon" (a dictator), "The Silence" (a man pretending to be rich makes a greedy man slit his throat), and "The Masks" (a rich man takes revenge on his haughty relatives). Those episodes not written by Serling continue this theme ("The Bewitchin' Pool," "Spur of the Moment," "A Piano in the House," "Queen of the Nile") with all featuring rich and scheming people.[8] Even equality is seen as boring and monotonous ("The Mind and the Matter").

Therefore, what can we conclude about Rod Serling's political theory and his view of human nature? What, for Serling, is the purpose of the state and the individual's relation to it? This is a question we must suspend for now until we have delved into the depths and nitty gritty of *The Twilight Zone*. Only then can we have a better understanding of these questions.

Chapter 1 will be a look at the Serling/Hobbesian state of nature. The "state of nature" was a rhetorical device used by the so-called social contract theorists of the seventeenth century to explain the origins of society and government. In particular, the Hobbesian state of nature, based on the writings and theories of the seventeenth-century English political philosopher Thomas Hobbes, saw man as belligerent, acquisitive, and self-interested. Serling, too, focuses on these themes—man's inhumanity to man, the need for compassion. Without a conscience or the rule of law do humans degenerate to their natural state for both Hobbes and Serling? For both, they must rise above their basic nature. But how?

Chapter 2 will look at political power and the state. Is the state liable to abuse power as much as use it? Does the state instill conformity which leads to, in the words of Alexis de Tocqueville "Tyranny of the Majority"? How does this play out in the world of Rod Serling's *Twilight Zone*? War and capital punishment are also considered.

Chapter 3 will consider fascism and modernity and what it means to Serling in *The Twilight Zone*. Serling generally does not like modernity which brings with it things like the atom bomb, automation, and bad architecture. Many of his stories hark back to happier and simpler times when people and neighbors were friendlier, when there was no "rat race." Such episodes as "A Stop at Willoughby," "A Thing about Machines" and "No Time Like the Past" illustrate this. For Serling, fascism is seen as the most negative aspect of modernity.

The conclusion considers whether Serling's dark view of the world leaves some hints of optimism—the human spirit, the magical or unexplained that makes Earth a habitable planet after all.

Notes

1. *TV Guide*, August 1, 2004.
2. John Bolton, quoted in *NY Daily News*, Sept 22, 2007, p. 4.
3. "The Dick Cavett Show," July 17, 1972.

4. Horace Mann was Antioch's first president and this quote is from his commencement speech to the class of 1858.

5. Hobbes, Thomas, *Leviathan*, ch. 13.

6. Serling, *Twilight Zone*, "The Monsters Are Due on Maple St."

7. In the episode "The Fear" a woman is afraid of aliens and asks a police officer to protect her. The state can achieve power through fear—but in this case the alien is only a large balloon and the aliens are small.

8. "Spur of the Moment," by Richard Matheson, features rich people (slightly but not much) more favorably.

1

Human Nature

Nothing is so much to be feared as fear.

—Henry Thoreau

A LL POLITICAL PHILOSOPHERS HAVE a view of human nature which is the foundation of their political theories and ideas about the state. Serling agreed saying that humanity was his business.[1] A benevolent view of human nature will lead to a different kind of political philosophy than a negative view of human nature. What is Serling's view? Serling, like Hobbes, has expressed a decidedly negative view of human nature in *The Twilight Zone*, one that shows humans as belligerent, appetitive, acquisitive and self interested.

"The Fever" is illustrative of Serling's view that humans are appetitive and acquisitive and this can be a negative influence. In "The Fever" Mr. And Mrs. Franklin Gibbs arrive in Las Vegas for a trip that is a prize in a contest Mrs. Gibbs has won. The scene is ominous. Photographers set upon the Gibbses in order to take a picture of them for their hometown newspaper—but when Mrs. Gibbs tells the photographer the name of the newspaper—the Elgin Bugle—he seems confused. This is not a photo for the newspaper at all—it's as if a photo is needed to document who these people are in case something happens to them—something bad. The photographer reminds them they have "unlimited credit."

"The Fever" refers to the obsessive gambling that takes hold of Franklin Gibbs even though he sees it as immoral. When he sees a basket of cash handed out to a jackpot winner he becomes a gambling fiend, even after scolding his wife about playing a nickel slot machine. On his way back to his room Franklin gets waylaid by a drunk and overcomes his distaste for gambling long enough to play the slot machine and win. Now that Franklin has been corrupted by the "baboons" he can hardly tear himself away. He hears a voice—his inner conscience, what Hobbes would call appetite—calling him back to the machine. He can't sleep—the voice calls to him at night—visions of quarters play in his mind and he is consumed with greed. In order to get rid of the "dirty" money he goes back to feed it into the slot machine. The machine, says Franklin, "teases you. It holds out promises and wheedles you. It sucks you in."

This is reminiscent of Tocqueville's view of the American Dream. It's a hoax—yet Americans are so ambitious and acquisitive that they keep running the "race of life" and are "always in a hurry" "upon the pursuit of worldly welfare."[2] Franklin gambles all night and he says "it's got to pay off. Sooner or later it's got to." But, as Tocqueville says about the American Dream, it doesn't. Franklin breaks the slot machine and flies into a rage of greed and obsession. A casino worker hangs a sign "out of order" on the slot machine. Not only is it out of order but Franklin Gibbs is out of order, overcome by his greed and obsession just as Americans are overcome by their ambition to achieve the "American Dream" of status.[3]

A machine has turned on modern man. Franklin hears voices again and sees the slot machine pursuing him. It has a smiling lighted mouth and calls to him. The machine forces him out the window. One quarter falls just out of his reach, just as the American Dream is just out of reach.[4] The slot machine is something that has power to do you good or harm, it's a game of chance like the American Dream—theoretically open to all but really closed to most.

The same combination of obsession and appetite is seen in "Nick of Time," written by Richard Matheson, where a machine becomes the devil that tempts Don Carter into appetitiveness. A young honeymoon couple is driving to New York when their car breaks down in Ohio. It will take three or four hours to fix the car so they decide to have lunch at a diner. Don Carter, played by William Shatner, shows that he is superstitious when he says "bread and butter" while holding his wife's hand as they walk by a post in the road. This irrationality sets the scene for the rest of the story, as do a rabbit's foot and four leaf clover keychain.

In the diner, much of the filming is done through a lattice work which gives an eerie impression that something demonic has taken hold—the couple is at odds or crossed purposes fighting between rationality (represented by Don's wife) and irrationality and appetite (represented by Don). The lattice work reminds us of prison bars that symbolize the body as the prison house of the soul (Plato) wherein rational people are imprisoned by their appetites and obsessions, or the spider web in which the Carters are trapped.

They sit down at a booth and put money into a "mystic seer" fortune teller machine with a devil's head on top of it. Mr. Carter asks the machine questions about his future such as whether he will be promoted. The machine says yes, and when he calls his office the secretary tells him he has been promoted to office manager. Carter can resist the "chicken fried steak" that the proprietor offers him and instead eats a sensible lettuce and tomato sandwich on whole wheat bread, but he cannot resist the temptation of the mystic seer machine to tell his fortune. This "appetite" or "endeavor" is what Hobbes says fuels human nature, perhaps especially in the state of nature, from *Leviathan* chapter six. Of Man: "This Endeavour, when it is toward something . . . is called Appetite . . . and when the Endeavor is fromward something, it is generally called Aversion. . . ."

The machine tells them to stay in the diner until 3 o'clock and suggests that if they leave before then something bad will happen to them. They stay in the diner imprisoned behind the lattice work until 3 o'clock. At that point Mrs. Carter insists they leave. Don allows a "napkin holder in a little café in Ridgeview, Ohio" to control his life. In the street they almost get hit by a car. Don looks at the town clock and it is exactly 3 o'clock.

Now, more convinced than ever that the "mystic seer" can see his fortune, Don goes back to the diner and two other customers are sitting in the booth previously occupied by them—now they are imprisoned with the mystic seer behind the lattice work. Mrs. Carter is afraid that Don has lost his free will to superstition and obsessive appetite. Is success based on luck and fortune or hard work and talent? Is there free will? Mrs. Carter starts to cry and they leave the diner, as another couple enters and goes to the mystic seer. Now they are imprisoned in the lattice work and ask "do you think we might leave Ridgeview today?" Serling's voiceover says "Two people enslaved by the tyranny of fear and superstition, facing the future with a kind of helpless dread" while the Carters have escaped the spider's web of fear and superstition.

Perhaps the most Hobbesian man is Arthur Castle in "The Man in the Bottle" who wants glory, wealth and power. Mr. Castle owns a junk/antique store and is going broke until a lady brings him an old bottle for which he generously gives her a dollar. The bottle falls on the floor and a genie comes out and offers the Castles three wishes. First, Mr. Castle makes a small wish—to fix the broken showcase glass. When this is fulfilled he goes on to a bigger wish.

Mr. Castle's next wish is for money—$1 million. Money falls from the ceiling but they give it away and owe the tax collecter. Once they see how fast money goes they want something else.

Mr. Castle next wishes for power—to be the head of a foreign country who can't be voted out of office in the twentieth century—he is turned into Hitler. Finally, he wishes he were Arthur Castle and is back in his shop. Now he appreciates his store. His appetites got him into trouble. He did get a new showcase out of the deal—until, while sweeping up the broken bottle, Arthur hits the showcase with the broom handle and breaks it again.

What does this have to do with human nature and Hobbes?

The State of Nature—Hobbesian Roots

In order to understand what these elements have to do with Serling's view of human nature we must look at the rhetorical device used by social scientists and philosophers known as the State of Nature. Used by the so-called Social Contract theorists, notably Hobbes, Locke, and Rousseau—but others too— the state of nature allowed social scientists to study human nature by seeing what humans would be or were like without government. To do this, social contract theorists imagined a time and place before government or the creation of "the state" when humans were most primitive. Think of it in terms of cavemen, or the jungle—where humans are simply ruled by their impulses.

With no state to control humans, what impulses are they controlled by? Hobbes says in the state of nature one main impulse—fear, or "diffidence"—controls humans. Thus, fear is the overwhelming impulse of humans, in particular fear of violence. But other impulses control humans too—Hobbes says "glory" and "greed" are also key to understanding human nature in the state of nature. If these three impulses play out in the state of nature according to Hobbes, how do these themes play out in the characters and themes of the *Twilight Zone*?[5]

Fear

> Something's in the air. . . . Everyone's afraid. . . .
>
> —Jody Sturka, "Third from the Sun"

As a theme, fear is almost as pervasive in Rod Serling's view of the world in *The Twilight Zone* as it is in Hobbes' political philosophy. We could go back into the Antioch College records and see if Serling ever took political philosophy, if in fact he read Hobbes or any of the social contract theorists or some of the more pessimistic philosophers such as Malthus, because Serling's view of human nature is as shaped by the motivation of fear as is any philosopher's view of human nature. Fear of the unknown, fear of the sinister, fear of violence and—for Serling—fear of nuclear war. This theme, fear, perhaps more than any other, is the glue that holds *The Twilight Zone* together as a cohesive piece of work. Bunny Blake replies to her assistant in "The Ring-a-Ding Girl," when she asks if she's afraid, "isn't everyone?"

What then is there to be afraid of?

Ourselves, first of all. This is demonstrated vividly in "The Monsters Are Due on Maple St.," a show associated with the serenity of rural life that includes violent undertones for which Serling is famous. The opening scene is ideal suburbia—reminiscent of Serling's childhood in Binghamton, New York—the voiceover says "a tree lined little world of front porch gliders, barbeques, the laughter of children and the bell of an ice cream vendor. This is Maple St. in the last calm reflective moment before the monsters came." The lights go out, the phones go out. The neighbors gather to discuss the power outage. The cars won't work. A boy claims to have seen a UFO. He plants an idea that aliens have sent down scouts "who look just like humans" but aren't.

Now the neighbors look at each other with suspicion. A neighbor's car starts by itself. They are suspicious of him and call him an "oddball." Another neighbor, Steve, cautions them not to be a mob. Steve expresses concerns about monsters from outer space as the car starts by itself again. One of the neighbors says she saw Les Goodman in the middle of the night standing on his porch waiting for something. He calls them "scared, frightened rabbits." Another neighbor, Charlie, says "under normal circumstances I'd let it go by but these aren't normal circumstances."

Charlie and Steve start yelling and accusing each other. Steve says they are eating each other up. They hear footsteps. The boy says "it's the monster." Someone shoots another neighbor. It was dark—he didn't know he wasn't the monster. The lights start going on in Charlie's house. Now they suspect Charlie. He runs away, the neighbors run after him with rocks. Charlie says the boy is the monster. The boy and his mother start to run. The neighbors accuse each other and there is a "war of all against all" or Hobbes' war "of every man against every man." From high above two aliens are watching the chaos: "Just stop a few of their machines throw them into darkness for a few hours, sit back and watch the pattern." The other alien responds "and this pattern is always the same?" "With few variations. They pick the most dangerous enemy they can find and it's always themselves. All we need do is sit back and watch." The second alien says "then I take it this place, this Maple St., is not unique?" "By no means. Their world is full of Maple Streets. And we'll go from one to the other and let them destroy themselves. From one to the other, one to the other" as they board their spaceship. Serling says "there are weapons that are simply thoughts, attitudes, prejudices to be found only in the minds of men. Prejudices can kill and suspicion can destroy. And a thoughtless frightened search for a scapegoat has a fallout all its own. And the pity of it is that these things cannot be confined to the Twilight Zone."

So Serling understands that fear, diffidence, prejudice and violence are "found only in the minds of men" and are part of human nature. This is the human nature of Hobbes. As Scott's alien supervisor tells him in "Black

Leather Jackets," written by Earl Hamner, Jr., the world is one of fearful and angry people.

Fear also plays an important role in Serling's "It's A Good Life," based on a short story by Jerome Bixby, which explains how people tyrannize themselves through the use of fear and how violence supplements it. The scene is a rural farm in Ohio where there is a monster. The monster is a little boy named Anthony Fremont. Anthony has the power to make it snow, to turn people into animals and vice versa. In particular he does not like singing. Anthony sends anyone who sings into the cornfield. Everyone is afraid of Anthony because he has these powers.

At a birthday party for a neighbor the neighbor is given a Perry Como record. But Anthony says he cannot play it. The response from the neighbors is "it's good that he can't play the record. It's real good." This is the response to anything Anthony says. The neighbor, Dan, says to Anthony's parents "You. You and her you had him. You hadda go have him. You monster. You murderer. You think bad thoughts about me" and Anthony replies "you're a bad man. You're a very bad man." Dan says "somebody sneak up behind him. Somebody end this." Anthony puts Dan's head on a jack in the box, puts him into the cornfield and warns the rest of the neighbors not to think "bad thoughts" about him or he'll "do the same thing" to them. Anthony makes it snow which will ruin the crops. But everyone decides "it's good you're making it snow."

Anthony is a dictator and this is the way fascism works, through fear and violence.

One aspect of fear that pervades *The Twilight Zone* is fear of nuclear war, a theme that is played out in several shows including two classic episodes "The Shelter" and "Time Enough at Last." "The Shelter" starts, as do most of Serling's shows, with a happy scene of a birthday party. But it's always doomsday in *The Twilight Zone* and it quickly becomes sinister. A suburban party, laughter, a birthday cake, a toast about how much these neighbors love each other. The party is for Dr. William Stockton, the well respected neighborhood family doctor. In the midst of the festivities Dr. Stockton's son reports to the guests that "four minutes ago the president of the United States reported radar evidence of UFOs" and there is "a state of yellow alert." The civil defense authorities ask everyone to move to a shelter. The guests run out of the house, and the neighborhood looks sinister. Rod Serling appears and says "what you are about to watch is a nightmare." The doctor has a shelter in his basement that he has been working on. He goes about preparing it for his wife and son. This is a New York suburb. The doctor says "with any luck" they'll survive in the shelter.

The neighbors realize they do not have shelters, and one by one they return to the doctor's house. The first neighbor, Jerry, wants to bring his family to the shelter but it can only hold three people. The doctor says "it's my family I have to worry about. I kept telling you—build a shelter. Admit to yourself the worst was possible." The next neighbor is Marty, he is with his wife and two infants. He appeals to the doctor to let him into the shelter. The doctor calls to him from inside the shelter saying he can't and he won't. Marty says "you'll survive but you'll have blood on your hands. You're a doctor—you're supposed to help people." The doctor tells Marty to get out.

A third neighbor, Frank, wonders why they don't break the door down. The neighbors outside the shelter start to argue. Marty suggests the doctor pick one family to let in the shelter. Frank says "that's the way it is when the foreigners come over here—pushy, grabby." They start fighting. Jerry says they're a mob. Frank hits Marty.

Inside the shelter the doctor's wife says "Bill, who are those people?" The neighbors batter down the door just as the president announces that the UFOs are satellites and there are no enemy missiles approaching. The state of emergency has been called off. Frank says to Marty "I went off my rocker." The neighbors offer to pay for the damage to the shelter with a block party so they can "get back to normal." The doctor wonders "what normal is" and if they know what the "damages are. Maybe one of them is finding out what we're really like underneath the skin. We were spared a bomb tonight but I wonder if we weren't destroyed even without it." Serling says "for civilization to survive the human race must remain civilized." Serling, like Hobbes, understood that humans are only civilized under the threat of compulsion. If the world is going to blow up there is no compulsion so humans revert to their natural state—belligerent, acquisitive, pugnacious and violent.

"The Fear" focuses on the human fear of the unknown, "diffidence" in this case with the use of Serling's favorite theme of aliens. The story considers a woman from the city who has come to a rural cabin to get off the treadmill of the urban rat race—another Serling theme. Miss Charlotte Scott has moved to a small town from New York , but she still has the chain latched on her cabin door. Trooper Franklin comes to her house to investigate a UFO sighting. She has seen some strange lights. She had a nervous breakdown and came to the cabin to be alone.

As trooper Franklin is about to leave they see the lights again. Trooper Franklin asks "you're not frightened, are you Miss Scott?" She replies "I'm the founder and chairman of the board of a society of frightened people. So frightened that they can't face the world. And they go away to little mountain retreats." After something moves trooper Franklin's car he goes back into the cabin and instructs Miss Scott, a former fashion editor, to put the chain on the door. She says "you've just applied for membership, hmm? My club for frightened people."

Franklin confesses in his line of work he's "racked up more scared hours than most rabbits." He says "being frightened is a normal, natural human function just like breathing. It's how you react to fright that's what really counts." Miss Scott threatens to hide "under the bed" he says "you got two beds? I might like to do a little crawling under one of them myself."

The invader must stand more than 500 ft. They see a big footprint, presumably left by the alien—but the "alien" is only a balloon. The aliens are in a small spaceship and report back to their leader the mission failed because of "Earth men's failure to be frightened." The aliens are now afraid of *them*, and leave Earth. Franklin says "maybe the next place they land, they can be the giants." Miss Scott says "what if our next visitors . . . what if they are giants?" Serling's voiceover says that the worst thing we have to fear, is fear itself.

"The Fear" has a somewhat optimistic message: Miss Scott stays and faces her fears and sees they turn out to be unjustified. Serling's message is, perhaps, if we face fears they are not so frightening, and the worst thing is to be paralyzed by fear which is a core element of human nature. Or, as Hobbes says, fear leads us to do good things like establish government (represented by trooper Franklin) to protect us.

The idea that fear may halt progress is demonstrated in "The Gift" which is set in Mexico. A UFO has crashed into the hills of a rural village. The police officer who witnessed the crash fired shots and seems to think he saw a "monster." The doctor in the village says "you have frightened all these people—I just want to make sure that the source of the fear is not an illusion." Pedro is a boy who works at the café where the doctor is drinking. He is not afraid of the UFO and the proprietor of the café considers this strange.

As the doctor is about to leave the café a stranger wanders in asking for wine. The proprietor is frightened of the stranger which makes the stranger hit him over the head with a bottle. The stranger explains that he came in peace but the townspeople are so afraid of him that they try to kill him. The stranger says the only person "who feels neither fear nor anger" is Pedro. Pedro says he feels like an outsider too.

The stranger directs Pedro to "a gift" which is in a book he brought with him. Pedro helps the doctor take care of the wounded stranger, who refuses painkillers, and says "he is my friend." The doctor takes bullets out of the stranger who is superhuman—he has been shot but is strong. The doctor got to him hours too late—obviously he is not human.

The proprietor fears the stranger and wants to turn him into the police. Pedro comforts the stranger who wonders why "men fear the unknown." Pedro confesses he is an "odd one." They are both odd. The gift represents that the stranger came "as a visitor not an invader" and Pedro wonders about good people who have been the object of fear by ignorant people, and who have been killed. The stranger says that "soon people will not be afraid and then I can show them the gift."

But Serling is not as optimistic as the stranger. Just then the police drive up. One brags about shooting the stranger. "If he is only one man . . . why do you need us?" asks another policeman. The doctor warns the police the stranger cannot be moved, but when they go to look for him they can't find him. The village is in a panic but the stranger says "I come in peace." They corner him. He asks Pedro to show them the gift. The villagers set fire to the book and kill the stranger as he goes toward Pedro.

The stranger lies in a heap while the doctor puts out the fire and picks up the book which says "Greetings to the people of Earth. We come as friends and in peace. We bring you this gift. The following chemical formula is a vaccine. It's a vaccine against all forms of cancer." The rest of the book was burned.

The villagers stand around looking at each other and the doctor takes Pedro home. Serling's voiceover says: "Madeiro, Mexico, the present. The subject: fear. The cure: a little more faith. An Rx off a shelf in the Twilight Zone." So, while for Hobbes fear can motivate us to do good (i.e., move into government and seek peace) it can also prevent us from seeking peace and from progress that can be of great use to humanity. Keep in mind this is the flip side of the message in "To Serve Man" where "more faith" resulted in Mr. Chambers becoming "an ingredient" in an alien's soup.

Jackie Rhodes is a character wrapped in the mantel of fear and embodies fear perhaps more than any of Serling's characters. "Nervous Man in a Four Dollar Room" opens in a dingy hotel room where Jackie sits biting his nails. He is a two bit small time criminal in league with gangsters from whom he takes orders. Jackie's life has been given over to "fighting adversaries" of whom he is afraid and one of those adversaries is him. He is sweating and worried and looks "as if during each ensuing hour he had a dentist appointment" as Serling says of Barbara in "Uncle Simon."

Jackie is bedeviled by phantoms real and imaginary. He is nervous especially when his boss, a sophisticated thug named George, comes to give him his marching orders. Jackie is afraid that his next assignment may land him in jail. George gives him a gun and asks him to kill a saloon owner who won't pay bribes. Jackie is afraid to do it—"I got no guts" he tells George. George threatens Jackie not to "chicken out" so Jackie is afraid to do the assignment and afraid not to do it.

As Jackie considers his options he has a conversation with himself in the mirror in which a more courageous Jackie speaks. Jackie asks himself in the mirror "why am I scared? Why am I all the time scared?" He's a "scared, nervous little nail biter" to whom the more courageous Jackie speaks, whom he describes as "cheap, weak, scared" and whom he watches as he faints on the bed.

The good Jackie tells the scared Jackie that he was afraid of everything—the street gang that made him turn to crime, of marrying Janie Reardon, etc. This is Jackie's fearful side fighting with his rational side.

Jackie's rational side wins and he doesn't go to do the assignment. When George confronts him about it he hits George and resigns. His rational self has won. He is no longer motivated by fear, he checks out of the $4 room and has stopped biting his nails. This is an optimistic view that the rational can win over the fearful, that we can govern ourselves in theory and practice, and that when we organize ourselves we can organize government.

"Nightmare as a Child" is the flipside of "Spur of the Moment"—in "Nightmare" a teacher named Helen Foley is haunted by herself as a child nineteen years earlier, and in "Spur," written by Richard Matheson, an equestrian is haunted by herself in the future.

Nightmare is a story of pervasive fear in which Helen and a girl named Markie are frightened by a man who used to work for Helen's mother. Something happened to Helen, her mother was murdered when she was a child and she has amnesia. The man, Peter Selden, looks familiar and stalks her and says "I had quite a crush on you."

Selden tells Helen that Markie was her nickname. He shows her a picture of herself as a child and it's the girl Helen is haunted by. Selden confesses that he killed her mother because she was going to turn him over to the police. He grabs Helen but falls down the stairs. The policeman says the child is a "recollection" and "the human imagination is often weird."[6]

"The Jungle" (by Charles Beaumont) demonstrates the fate of those not motivated by fear as does "The Grave." In "The Jungle" the protagonist (John Dehner) is fearless and criticizes superstition then pays for his foolish lack of fear. In "The Grave" Conny Miller (Lee Marvin) is also fearless and is also penalized for it, thus demonstrating that, as Hobbes said, fear motivates us and it is unwise to deny it.

The scene is New York City in a swank apartment. Alan Richards, an industrialist, questions his wife about her African souvenirs which are the "baubles of a witch doctor" and he throws them in the fire over her protests. He reminds her that they are in New York not Africa and good luck charms are "for weak people, ignorant uncivilized people who don't know any better ... what are you afraid of?"

His wife is afraid that the industrialists have "wounded the land" according to the African shaman—and the land would "make us pay." Alan says he's an engineer working on a hydroelectric project and he does not "pander to ignorant witch doctors." These are wealthy people—the painting over the fireplace mantel looks like a Klimt. Alan's wife asks him not to go to the industrialist meeting but he opens the door to go and sees the carcass of a goat in the hallway.

Alan goes to the Board of Directors meeting anyway where someone asks about "the natives" and Richards says "they resent us" but mentions the shaman curse "uchowie" witchcraft. Now he speaks as a believer saying "I've seen it work." Now he's a critic—he sees that Mr. Sinclair is wearing a rabbit's foot, Mr. Hardy believes in astrology and "allows the stars to make his decisions." Mr. Temple knocks on wood, Mr. Fleming won't walk under a ladder, etc. Richards mocks them saying they're ignorant and allowing the company to be "run by witches" and notes that their building doesn't even have a 13th floor."

After the meeting Richards sits drinking at a bar and sees a lion's tooth and "amulet" to protect him from lions. Richards laments that superstition and fear are destroying civilization. He makes the mistake of leaving the lion's tooth at the bar. When he goes to his car at 3 a.m. it won't start. He goes back to the bar but it's closed. The camera focuses on the tooth on the bar.

Richards goes to a phone booth to call his wife but it's broken and all he hears are noises of the jungle. He starts to walk home and feels a sirocco or jungle wind whipping up. He gets in a taxi and the driver falls over. He gets out of the taxi and runs, sees a tribal warrior with a spear in a costume shop. He gives a vagrant money to walk with him but the vagrant doesn't hear the jungle noises. He sees ornamental lion statues and hears a lion roar. He runs home through the park, gets to his building and his apt, and pours himself a drink. When he opens his bedroom door there is a real lion on his bed that lunges at him. The moral: "there are things that are not dreamt of in your philosophy, Horatio" it pays to be afraid. Richards becomes afraid of the jungle too late to protect himself.

The Hobbesian theme that fear protects us in a violent world is also demonstrated in "Twenty-Two," "The Howling Man" and "Nightmare at 20,000 Feet."

In "Twenty-Two" a woman (Liz Powell) is in a hospital bed in a dark room. She is afraid. She walks into the hallway and gets on the elevator. She has a nightmare about the number 22 and a woman saying "room for one more." For Serling, it's strange that he connects fear to airplanes frequently—as in "Twenty-Two" and "Nightmare at 20,000 Feet" because he was a flying enthusiast. However, in these portrayals he is demonstrating a ubiquitous fear. When Liz is released she goes to board the plane to go home and it's flight 22—the stewardess is the same woman from the dream and she says "room for one more." Liz runs away and the plane blows up—her fear protects her.

The fear of airplanes as "irrational" is also shown in "Nightmare at 20,000 Feet" (written by Richard Matheson) where Bob Wilson (William Shatner) is returning home on a plane after a nervous breakdown (which was on a plane). He is scared. The plane was where he had his breakdown and why he was in a "sanitarium" As the plane door closes he confesses to his wife to "a little abject cowardice."

Serling's voiceover introduces the piece: "portrait of a frightened man." Mr. Wilson looks out the window and sees a yeti or abominable snowman on the wing. But nobody believes him especially since he was just released from the "sanitarium." Everyone's (the stewardess, his wife, the flight engineer) lack of fear puts the plane in jeopardy.

The yeti (he calls it a "gremlin") is outside the plane during a storm trying to tear a hole in the plane or tamper with an engine. When Mr. Wilson asks his wife to call the flight engineer, the flight engineer acts like Mr. Wilson is crazy. What is he to do?

The gremlin pulls up a metal plate on the plane but the flight engineer says to the stewardess "don't worry, Betty, everything's fine." They are not afraid. Wilson grabs a gun from a passenger's holster. He opens the auxilliary exit, hangs out the plane and shoots the yeti. The men in white coats take him off the plane—but he saved the flight. Serling's voiceover says "happily" Mr. Wilson's belief will not remain his own, for "tangible manifestation is very often left as evidence of trespass" even in *The Twilight Zone* and they show the metal panel pulled up on the plane.

A family is protected by fear in "Third from the Sun." Bill Sturka and his family leave their planet because there is going to be a nuclear war. Mr. Sutrka goes home from the plant where he works and tells his family they must leave in 48 hours. The house is contemporary in the style of the nuclear age. Their daughter, Jody, says "something's going to happen and everybody's afraid. . . ." Bill replies "people are afraid because they make themselves afraid." He explains that people "subvert" great inventions (like the hydrogen bomb that he works on). But their fear saves them from the planet's nuclear war and they leave on a spaceship. On the spaceship they wonder about the planet they are going to—"it's the third planet from the sun, Bill, it's called 'Earth.' That's where we're going to a place called Earth."

In "The Howling Man" (written by Charles Beaumont) Brother Jerome's fear protects him and the world—in contrast to David Ellington's lack of fear.

A man named David Ellington seeks refuge in a European hermitage or castle of the "Brothers of Truth" on a stormy night—he is lost and wants shelter. At first they say "no" but he collapses and they take him in.

The hermitage is inhabited by a hermit sect led by Brother Jerome. Ellington hears a howling and sees a howling man locked in a jail who begs to be let out and explains that Brother Jerome has enslaved him there. Brother Jerome takes Ellington aside and explains to him that the man in the jail is "the devil himself" who they have kept cooped up for five years. There was peace in the world for five years between WWI and WWII.

But Ellington is not afraid of the howling man—he takes the key from the brother who has fallen asleep and unlocks the jail. The devil walks out and wreaks havoc on the world. Ellington regrets that he was not afraid (he tells Brother Jerome he didn't recognize him and Jerome says "that is man's weakness and satan's strength") and makes it his mission to recapture him—which he does, and locks him in a closet in his home until the cleaning lady, through lack of fear, lets him out. The scene where the howling man becomes the devil is memorable—in each frame he becomes more and more devil-like, and at the end has horns. Lack of fear gets you in trouble. It got Mr. Chambers in trouble in "To Serve Man."

The fears of senior citizens is the theme of "Ninety Years without Slumbering" and "Nothing in the Dark." In "Ninety Years," written by Richard deRoy (based on a story attributed alternately to Johnson Smith and George Clayton Johnson) Ed Wynn plays Sam Forstmann who we see singing a traditional song "My Grandfather's Clock."[7] Sam lives with his granddaughter and wakes up in the middle of the night afraid that the grandfather clock will stop. The clock was a gift the day he was born and he fears that if it stops he will die. Serling tells us that some men measure their time by fear—Sam's father also had "Ninety Years without Slumbering" because he was afraid the clock would stop.

Sam's granddaughter and her husband believe this is an irrational fear that is controlling Sam and send him to their friend, a psychiatrist, who wonders why Sam is so interested in the clock. Sam tells the psychiatrist that if the clock stops he'll die. First, they try to move the clock out of Sam's room to the hallway. When the pendulum stops he faints on the stairs. Then, he decides to sell the clock to a neighbor, but he's still obsessed with visiting the clock every day. When he looks in the neighbor's window and sees the pendulum slowing he breaks the window and the police see him. They bring him home and he goes to bed. As the pendulum slows, Sam's soul leaves his body and talks to him. This is one of the most spectacular effects in *The Twilight Zone*—a man having a conversation with his soul.[8]

Sam's spirit wants to go, but Sam argues with the spirit—a reference to *A Christmas Carol* which was a favorite of Serling—and says he used to believe the story about the clock but it's silly because he's been to a psychiatrist and he lives "in the present" and plans to keep living in the present.[9] Sam states that if he doesn't believe in ghosts then they don't exist and the spirit vanishes. Sam goes to sleep—his granddaughter wakes him up—and he's cured.

If we don't believe in our fears they don't have power. Now Sam's taking care of his granddaughter, Marnie, rather than the clock. He tells her that he thinks he overcharged the neighbor because the clock stopped and when it stopped he was "born again."

Fear rules the life of the lady in "Nothing in the Dark," written by George Clayton Johnson, and the moral is that you can run but your fears will find you even if you stay in your house. Fear controls us, even though you try to barricade out the thing you fear, as you run from it you run right into it.

The scene is an old woman's apartment. It snows outside, symbolic of the dreary atmosphere of her psyche. She looks through the bars of her bed, a prison of her own making. Someone outside is shot and needs help, but she is afraid to open the door. She is afraid of the grim reaper. She opens the door on a chain and sees a young man, Robert Redford, lying on the ground. He's a policeman and he's been shot. She takes him in. His name is Harold Beldon.

The woman's apartment is barricaded and she is a prisoner of her fear. But as much as you barricade, the objects of your fear don't come in the package you think they will—Harold is young and handsome—who better to trick and con you? Our fears are rational, according to Hobbes but, as Plato said about courage, we don't always know what to fear. Because our fears are familiar to us, we let them in. As Sam said—if I don't believe the fear it doesn't exist and the more your phobias pen you in the more likely they are to control you—we tend to attract what we fear. Robert Redford tells the lady there's nothing to fear but, in truth, as Bunny Blake said in "The Ring-a-Ding Girl," "everyone's afraid."

A man breaks the door down—he's going to demolish the tenement to make room for a new building. The lady is like the tenement. The more we run and hide the more our fears find us. The construction worker can't see Mr. Beldon—the lady looks in the mirror and she's not there. He tricked her. She says that she's afraid but she gives him her hand. She is now a spirit. Serling reminds us that our fears are there in the light, not just in the dark. Hobbes said that people are afraid, or "diffident" and Serling tells us that it controls those of all ages—"Nightmare as a Child," "The Fear," "The Monsters are Due on Maple St.," "It's A Good Life," and "The Hitch-Hiker."

Like "Ninety Years "and "Nothing in the Dark," "The Hitch-Hiker," based on a radio play by Lucille Fletcher, is a story about a woman, Nan Adams, who is haunted and pursued by fear as she drives from New York to Los Angeles. Her tire blows out and the mechanic says she is "on the side of the angels" and Serling says that her route is fear. A man follows her after the accident—he is the grim reaper who is hitch hiking across country. Nobody else sees him, like Harold Beldon in "Nothing in the Dark."

She keeps seeing the man, the hitch-hiker, and she is frightened when the man at the restaurant tells her there are no hitch-hikers there. She stops for construction and the hitch-hiker tries to get in the car. He almost makes her get stuck on the tracks and hit by a train. Should she turn around and go back? Should she continue?

She drives and drives, pursued by the hitch-hiker, she tries to escape but runs out of gas. She goes to a gas station, but it's closed. A sailor going back to San Diego tells the man to give her gas and she says she'll give him a ride to San Diego. She gets back in the car with the sailor and wonders how the hitch-hiker is always going faster than her. She sees the hitch-hiker and swerves the car. But the sailor doesn't see him. The sailor leaves the car and she asks him not to go.

She's outside a diner near Tucson and she calls home but is told that her mother had a nervous breakdown when Nan was killed in an accident—now she sees the man again sitting in the back seat of her car. He is like Harold Beldon in "Nothing in the Dark," invisible to everyone but her.

Greed

> Greed is seen as the motive of most capitalist actions, cruelty as its all too willing handmaiden, and hypocrisy as the mask capitalists wear to hide their motives and means from others.
>
> —Karl Marx, "Economic and Philosophic Manuscripts of 1844"

"The Rip Van Winkle Caper" illuminates the belligerence, egoism, greed and acquisitiveness of human nature.

Four men rob a train going from Fort Knox to Los Angeles and steal its cargo of gold. The leader, a scientist, will use intelligence and science to facilitate the crime. He devises a plan to put them into suspended animation for 100 years. First, he puts a trainload of people to sleep. In the first scene we see greed, competition and the use of science to facilitate the crime. The thieves seal themselves in glass containers—only three come out of suspended animation because a rock falls on one of them and breaks the seal.

They emerge in the year 2061. The leader says "greedy men are the most dreamless, the least imaginative, the stupidest" expressing the human quest for wealth and overt materialism which, perhaps, Serling found distasteful. In a Hobbesian way, they start to distrust each other and fall into "mutual animosity." One says "I wouldn't trust you with gold if it was filling in your own mother's tooth." The man he says this to promptly runs him over with a truck in an attempt to destroy him and he smiles as he does it—another greedy thief he doesn't have to compete with. The two remaining men trudge through the desert where gold is worthless and water is the currency.

The gold is heavy and weighs them down. The thief with water shakes down the other thief for gold—one drink for one bar of gold. The leader is now the subject because of the other thief's greater ingenuity and ruthlessness. The price is then raised to two bars of gold for one sip of water. This continues until the leader kills the thief with the water.

But all for naught because in 2061 gold is worthless because people invented a way to manufacture it. So you can have a great plan—but greed will ruin it. Serling's voiceover says "they died precisely the way they lived—chasing an idol across the sand . . . to wind up . . . worthless as the gold bullion they built a shrine to." So, like the Midas touch greed and gold become worthless. Again, greed and competition are shown to be important and often destructive aspects of human nature, as Hobbes said.

"The Man in the Bottle" features both greed and glory as key aspects of human nature. Arthur Castle owns a junk/antique store and he is going broke until a lady brings him an old bottle for which he charitably gives her a dollar.[10] The bottle falls on the floor and a genie comes out and offers them four wishes. At first Mr. Castle makes a small wish—to fix the broken showcase glass in his store. When wish number one is fulfilled Mr. Castle goes on to a bigger wish.

The next wish is for money—$1 million. Money falls from the ceiling but they give it away and owe the tax collector. When the money goes they want something else.[11] The genie tells them to watch out "for the consequences." Mr. Castle wishes for power—to be the head of a modern foreign country who can't be voted out of office and is turned into Hitler. Now he wants to be Arthur Castle again back in his shop. Now he appreciates what he has. His appetites for greed and glory got him in trouble, those being the principle aspects of human nature according to Hobbes. He didn't even get a new showcase out of the deal—while sweeping up the broken bottle he hits the showcase with the broom handle and breaks it again. He is back where he started.

"The Silence" presents another picture of greed and the compelling and destructive human pursuit of money. The scene is a snobby gentleman's club where a young man, named Mr. Tennyson, is monopolizing a conversation about the stock market. He is boring a few of the older gentlemen, one of whom is asleep in a comfortable leather chair. One of them is annoyed, and he speaks to his lawyer, who is conveniently at the club, about a wager. Apparently Mr. Tennyson has asked for a loan of $250,000, but the older man has a more interesting deal for the talkative Tennyson. His lawyer advises him there is nothing criminal in the wager.

As the waiter at the club hands Mr. Tennyson a note from Colonel Taylor, he is talking about how he could invest $250,000 in plastics. The colonel's wager is a bet for $500,000 that Tennyson cannot remain silent for a year. He will be placed in a glass room at the club and communicate in writing. The

Colonel dislikes Tennyson, whose voice is "intolerable" Rather than convince him to resign the club, he offers Tennyson a bribe to shut him up.

The colonel says Tennyson would do almost "anything for money" knowing that Tennyson is motivated by money, having spent his inheritance. Tennyson accepts the wager and the colonel promises him a check for the money if he wins the bet. Tennyson asks the colonel to have the check certified and placed on deposit, but the colonel acts insulted and says Tennyson will have to take his word that he has the money. Tennyson confesses to the colonel's lawyer of his desperate need for money because his wife "shops at Tiffany's" like it's "a supermarket."

Tennyson enters the glass room at the club. It is furnished like a living room with a television set. There are microphones all around but he is quiet. He is dressed in a robe and an ascot scarf. The waiter at the club serves him food. It is very comfortable. But as time goes by the colonel becomes distressed that Tennyson is winning the bet and offers him $1000 to call it off. Tennyson declines. The colonel taunts him with rumors about his wife and suggests that he leave and save his marriage. He offers him $5000 to call off the bet but Tennyson says "the bet stands."

Tennyson wins the bet and emerges from the room. Taylor's lawyer tells him "twelve months ago to the moment you destroyed youself, much as I told you you would." It becomes clear that Archie doesn't have the money to pay off the bet. Tennyson holds out his hand. Archie admits that he doesn't have the money to pay the bet. Tennyson takes off the ascot scarf he is wearing and reveals in a note that he knew he wouldn't be able to keep silent—so he had the nerves to his vocal chords severed. Tennyson wins the bet, but he loses because of his greed.

Two shows that feature greed are "Uncle Simon" and "The Masks." Uncle Simon refers to Simon Polk, a wealthy man. His niece Barbara takes care of him in his mansion and makes him hot chocolate in English bone china. He is abusive and calls her a "passionless vegetable" and asks why she stays. She says "I want to be compensated for 25 years of being shrieked at, insulted, berated, humiliated and stepped on like an old rug." Barbara is described by Serling as someone who "has lived her life as if during each ensuring hour she had a dentist appointment."

Uncle Simon is working on a science project that Barbara is curious about so she goes to the basement to see what he is building. They get into an argument and she says she came to take care of him 25 years ago when he was sick and immobile. He says "everything you did for me you did for greed. Greed. Greed so big, so thick, so heavy that it blotted out even the hatred inside you. Let me tell you something, you money sick drone . . . before that payoff you'll pay through every bone in your body."

They argue and he falls down the stairs. Barbara refuses to help him saying "as of right now I am going to reap." But Barbara is condemned—because of a stipulation that if she does not take care of his science project all the property goes to the state university—the science project is a mechanical man that takes on his personality and needs to be waited on and served hot chocolate in bone china. An attorney checks on the robot once a week and Barbara is where she was—as Serling's voiceover says "tonight's uncomfortable little exercise in avarice and automatons." Reward does not come without strings and greed does not come without revenge in *The Twilight Zone*.

Serling does not like the greedy aspect of human nature and seeks to have it retributed in his stories.

In "A Short Drink from a Certain Fountain" a man named Harmon is married to a woman who is 40 years younger than him and she wants his money. She's "brassy, conniving and covetous" and a "predatory little alley cat" according to Harmon's brother, a doctor who is working on an anti-aging system. Harmon wants his brother to try the serum on him. Because it is experimental the brother refuses, but agrees when he thinks Harmon is going to jump off the balcony of his penthouse. The next day Harmon is 20 years younger—and he keeps getting younger until he is a baby. The retribution for Flora is that she has to take care of him—now she is the old one and as Serling says "the worm has turned."[12] As Serling says in "The Execution" "justice can span years. Retribution is not subject to a calendar."

Retribution is also a main theme of "The Masks" which is set in New Orleans at Mardi Gras. A family is going to see their father and grandfather, Jason Foster, who is very rich and very sick. When we first see the family arriving at his mansion they are ordering around the servants. Paula, the granddaughter, cannot take herself away from the mirror. Wilfred, the son in law, asks the doctor if "the old boy is in bad shape." They go up to Jason's ornate bedroom and he makes it clear that he knows they are just there because he is very rich and sick and says to Wilfred "I think the only book you ever read was a ledger. I think if someone cut you open they would find a cash register." Paula is still looking in the mirror.

According to Serling, Jason ("a tired ancient") will get retribution on his greedy relatives. Jason explains that they are going to have a Mardi Gras party with masks made by "an old Cajun" that have "certain properties" and the trick to wearing them is trying to "select the mask that is the antithesis to what the wearer is." Wilfred's mask has "greed, avarice, cruelty." Emily's (his daughter) is a "self centered coward." Paula's mask is vanity and Wilfred, Jr.'s mask is a "dull, stupid clown." Jason's is a skull.

Jason explains that the family came to New Orleans to say goodbye and "start grabbing things from my shelves . . . you came to reap everything I've sown, to collect everything I've built . . . everything is yours . . . the four of you inherit everything I own, everything, money, house, property holdings, stocks, bonds . . ." but he includes a small "proviso" that they wear the masks until midnight or they'll only get car fare back home. (The same wording is seen in "Uncle Simon" when Barbara says "as of right now I am going to reap").

Jason starts to cough and says "now you can dig deep in the treasury." He slumps in his wheelchair and says "now you're all very rich." They put the masks on but when they take them off their faces have turned into the masks representing their true characters and providing revenge for Jason.

The characters in "A Most Unusual Camera" also get justice for their greed. Chester and Paula, two petty crooks who rob an antique store, are complaining that they got junk including an antique camera. Chester takes a picture of Paula sitting by the window in a hotel room where they stashed their loot and the picture is of her wearing a fur coat. Then they open up a suitcase with a fur coat in it and Paula puts on the coat that was in the picture.

The camera takes pictures of the future. The camera takes a picture of Paula's brother, and he comes to the door. Chester decides he wants to give the camera to humanity, Paula replies that humanity never did anything for them. Chester says "that's the way we are—everything for us." Just then Paula's brother Woodward turns on the TV to horseracing and Chester decides he would rather take the camera to the racetrack to take a picture of the winning board before the race. When Woodward says "what about humanity?" Chester replies "what did humanity ever do for us?"

They make a suitcase full of money at the racetrack. The room service waiter, Pierre, comes into their room and reads the French words on the camera "ten to an owner" so the camera only takes ten pictures and there are two more. They start to fight about what to do with the camera—it takes a picture of Paula with her hands up. They are in a state of war over resources. Chester pulls a knife on Woodward—they fight and both fall out the window (a favorite image for Serling which is included in "What's in the Box?" and "Perchance to Dream"). Now all the money is Paula's. She takes the last picture—the waiter, Pierre, comes back and starts to take her money. The last picture has more than two bodies—Paula goes to look and trips on the rug and falls out the window, and Pierre falls out too. Serling's voiceover says: "object known as a camera . . . but for the greedy the avaricious, the fleet of foot who can run a four minute mile so long as they're chasing a fast buck, it makes believe it's an ally—but it isn't at all, it's a beckoning come on for a quick walk around the block in the Twilight Zone." Again, the greedy are punished—as is Franklin in "The Fever" by falling out the window.

Glory

According to Hobbes, men fight each other for glory or reputation. Glory, along with diffidence and greed, rules the state of nature and is an important part of human nature for Hobbes and Serling. Arthur Castle seeks glory as does Peter Craig in "The Little People" and Somerset Frisby in "Hocus Pocus and Frisby."

In "The Little People" two astronauts land on a planet. Peter Craig is second in command and does not like to take orders and be "led around by the nose." William Fletcher, the commander, asks him what he hungers for and Craig replies "I'd like a whole lotta people at my elbow, the more the merrier . . . but I'd like them on my terms . . . I'd like to give the orders." When he says that he hears little noises. Craig finds a stream and does not tell Fletcher. He has found miniature people and a miniature civilization. Craig says "all my life I wanted to sit in front of the wagon and hold the reins."

The little people are scared so they do what Craig says, he is big and they are small. He has the advantage of size over them. He becomes a dictator, but not a benevolent dictator. He starts to step on the society to instill fear until Fletcher hits him. Fletcher fixes the spaceship so they can go back to Earth but Craig doesn't want to go. The little people have erected a monument to him "like the Egyptian slaves on the pyramids" or "the Lilliputians with Gulliver."

In return for glory Craig won't step on them. He holds a gun on Fletcher and says "this is a monotheistic society" and there is no room for Fletcher. He tells Fletcher to leave without him.

Fletcher leaves and Craig is left with the little people. He throws his helmet on them as "a reminder" not to anger him. He is giddy at his power until another spaceship comes with astronauts that are giants. Now Craig is afraid they will step on him. They crush him and throw him down. The little people pull down the statue they erected to Craig. Power is relative.[13]

Even though "Hocus Pocus and Frisby" (based on an unpublished story by Frederic Louis Fox) is a whimsical fantasy about a bombastic character, Mr. Frisby,who loves to tell tall tales, there is a message about human nature that agrees with that of Hobbes—men want glory.

Mr. Frisby is a "boy who cried wolf" character and colorful charlatan who owns Frisby's General Store billed as "The Gimbel and Macy's of Pitchville Flats" where he holds court, chews the fat and tells tall tales to his friends.

Frisby is a liar and he lies to bring himself glory. He has stories about winning World War I, having a doctorate in meteorology from the University of Witchita (where he "wrote a thesis at age 13 that's still used as standard text") winning a competition with computers, inventing the automobile, leading the D-Day invasion, getting a Rhodes Scholarship (which he pronounces like "rogues") and turning it down (he refused to bow to the Queen) and having degrees from 38 schools.

One night Frisby gets visited by aliens who invite him aboard their spaceship where they hold him prisoner. They believe his tall tales and that's why they have chosen him to pick his brain believing him to be the most intelligent person on Earth.

Frisby admits to them that he is a liar. The aliens, who wear human masks over their alien faces, don't understand what that means. They put Frisby in a room on the spaceship and are about to take off for their planet when Frisby starts playing his harmonica, the sound of which disables the aliens who let him go.

Frisby goes back to his store where his friends are waiting to give him a surprise party. They crown him "World's Greatest Liar" and he tells them the story of his alien abduction—all for glory. If Frisby is represented by Serling as everyman, then everyman wants glory. As Hobbes said it is one of the principal aspects of human nature.

Glory also motivates Mr. Lou Bookman in "One for the Angels." Mr. Bookman is a sidewalk pitchman, a "nondescript commonplace little man whose life is a treadmill built out of sidewalks." He sells mechanical men, among other things, and is very friendly with the neighborhood children.

Mr. Bookman is being stalked by "Mr. Death" who informs him that his departure is at midnight and who is visible only to Bookman. Mr. Death informs him that there are three categories that qualify for deferment: hardship cases, statesmen and scientists, and "unfinished business." Bookman claims qualification in the third category claiming that he never made a big pitch—"a pitch for the angels." The glorious pitch is very important to Bookman because it would mean that the children would be proud of him. It would mean his moment of glory. Mr. Death agrees to grant him a delay until he makes his pitch—so Bookman decides never to make a pitch again, that way he'll be safe. But Mr. Death says "since you won't come with me I've been forced to select an alternative."

Bookman hears a car screech—his little friend Maggie has been run over by a car. Now Maggie sees Mr. Death and Bookman says "you can't take her." Maggie lies in bed and the doctor won't know if she'll be ok until midnight. Bookman decides to sit on the stoop and not let Mr. Death into the building—that way he'll save Maggie, if he doesn't get in by midnight then "the whole timetable" would be off.

Bookman gives Mr. Death a pitch. He gives such a great pitch that Mr. Death misses his appointment with Maggie—at one minute after midnight he goes with Bookman. Bookman has achieved greatness by making the pitch that saved Maggie. He has achieved glory.

Hobbes says that people are driven by glory or reputation and seek to redress "any other sign of undervalue, either direct in their persons or by reflection in their kindred, their friends, their nation, their profession, or their name."[14] In "The Sixteen Millimeter Shrine" an aging movie star is "undervalued" in her name and her profession by a Hollywood movie producer. She takes revenge by retreating into the past.

Barbara Jean Trenton is an aging star "struck down by hit and run years" and "trying . . . to get the license number of fleeting fame." She sits in her Beverly Hills mansion watching her old movies. She twirls around the room when her manager, Dan, comes to tell her about a film role and says "oh, Danny, I hope it's a musical—oh, I'd love to dance again."

When the Hollywood producer tells her "you'll play a mother" she says "I don't play mothers" and "I also don't take bit roles." He has "undervalued" her in her reputation and profession and her vanity lashes out at him. He replies "you may think you're still the number 1 lady on the top of the heap" but in fact "you're just an aging" has-been.

Barbara retreats to her mansion where she is in all her glory. "This is my world, Dan—right in here" she tells her manager. She is the queen of her castle where she lives in past glory.

Barbara wants to see her friends from the past, particularly Jerry Hearndan who was the leading man from her films, so her manager invites him to the mansion. When he arrives he is not the dashing figure in an officer's uniform that Barbara remembers from their old movies. Jerry tells her his film career "went down the drain with my youth" and he runs supermarkets in Chicago. She realizes that her glory days are in the past—his visit demonstrates this and she tells him to "go away."

Barbara retreats more and more, she is trapped in the past, because that's where her glory is and she literally becomes trapped in her home theater and in her movie screen—the sixteen millimeter shrine. "Sic transit Gloria."

Glory is also the theme of "The Changing of the Guard" set at the Rock Spring school for Boys in Rock Spring, Vermont. Ellis Fowler is an elderly and pedantic schoolteacher as Serling says "a gentle, bookish guide to the young."

The scene finds him three days before the Christmas holiday. Fowler is called into the Headmaster's office where he is told by the Headmaster that he has been forced into retirement. Fowler feels useless and contemplates suicide because he feels like a failure, he accomplished nothing and "motivated nobody."

Fowler goes to the school with a gun he took from his desk and stops at the statue of Horace Mann (the founder of Antioch College, where Serling was a student). He is about to pull the trigger of his pistol when he is saved by the ringing of class bells.

He goes into the classroom and is greeted by ghosts of former students all of whom say their lives were enriched by Fowler's teachings. One was in the navy at Pearl Harbor, one conducted research on x-rays. A student named Artie Beechcroft comes forward and shows Fowler the Congressional Medal of Honor for fighting at Iwo Jima. Beechcroft says "it's partly yours" because "you taught me about courage." They have all remembered poems and virtues that Fowler has taught them—patriotism, courage, loyalty, ethics.

Fowler realizes that he has contributed to humanity and his glory comes from the contributions and achievements of his students. He goes home and watches snow fall—he is like Scrooge on Christmas. He now appreciates his glory and says he was an influence on his students and, to his housekeeper, that he helped them win victories so perhaps he can share in them according to the principles of Horace Mann.[15]

Glory comes to Professor Fowler at the 11th hour and keeps him afloat. The Headmaster of the Rock Spring School "undervalues" Fowler but it rolls off his back when he can appreciate his own glory.

Competition and Belligerence—The Race of Life

Competition is a key component of human nature, according to Hobbes.[16] For Rousseau this competition is a result of a society that emphasizes it. Both of these are apparent in *The Twilight Zone*—the human nature and social aspects of competition—and usually demonstrated with disastrous effect. Swimming pools, big houses, affluence, and the facade of comfort of the suburbs are shown as sinister icons that bespeak misery and futility. These shows include such classic episodes as "A Stop at Willoughby," "The Bewitchin' Pool," "Queen of the Nile" and others, all with the theme of the dark side of competition.

While Hobbes made it clear that competition is part of human nature, and that people compete for gain or glory or out of fear, he also made it clear that human nature has a "nasty" and "brutish" side and that humans are "automata" that compete for the sake of competition—not because they like it, but because they are compelled to do so, chapter 6 of *Leviathan* Of Man: "Continuall successe in obtaining those things which a man from time to time desireth, that is to say, continuall prospering, is that men call FELICITY; . . . For there is no such thing as . . . Tranquility of mind while we live here; because Life it selfe is but motion, and can never be without Desire, nor without Feare. . . ." The belligerent nature of man is very apparent in the work of Hobbes and Machiavelli. For both philosophers, humans had a nasty side that would come out when there was no government, when there was a weak government, or when there were scarce resources. Without government to restrain men, all that would restrain them was a "power to keep them in awe" according to Hobbes or an even weaker restraint, themselves, according to Machiavelli. This would not be very effective and therefore whenever there was a breakdown of government there would be civil war. But even an earthquake or some other natural disaster—flood or fire—could cause such a breakdown.

"The Midnight Sun" shows the Hobbesian state of nature where, in a state of chaos with the Earth having gone off its orbit and moving too close to the sun, people behave in a world without rules, government or order.

Lois Nettleton, who plays Norma, is painting. The temperature is 110 degrees. People are fleeing her apartment building to go north. When Norma goes to the store and brings home juice the landlady grabs it and says "I'm acting just like an animal, aren't I?" This is the Hobbesian state of nature where people fight for scarce resources. Hobbes says: "Hereby it is manifest that during the time men live without a common power to keep them all in awe, they are in that condition which is called war; and such a war as is of every man against every man" or the "bellum omnium contra omnes."[17]

The scarce resource is water, people act like animals when there is no "common power to keep them all in awe." Norma describes pandemonium at the store—running, grabbing. A bulletin comes over the radio that people should lock their doors and be prepared to defend themselves with weapons. The police force has gone to the highways and citizens remaining in New York may have to protect themselves from people on the prowl looking for food and water. When there is "no common power" i.e., the state, people must take the law into their own hands as Norma will see.

The landlady, Mrs. Bronson, asks Norma to "paint something cool" like a waterfall. The sun gets hotter and it's now 120 degrees. Water is becoming more scarce and Norma is walking around in her underwear.

A man breaks into Norma's apartment. He is crazed. Norma has a gun and is prepared to defend her territory (in the absence of a state people must defend themselves). The man terrorizes Norma and Mrs. Bronson. He takes Norma's gun. He drinks their water, the lack of which has driven him crazy. He asks their forgiveness and leaves.

Norma paints a waterfall. Mrs. Bronson says "there's one near Ithaca, New York" like it.[18] They become delirious from the heat. The thermometer breaks and the painting melts—but it's all a dream and Norma wakes up to a cold world where the people are trying to stay warm and the Earth is moving away from the sun. Serling calls this "the poles of fear." Once again, fear and competition reign in a world without government and scarce resources. If it's not global warming it's nuclear winter.

The fight for resources or the struggle for freedom are Hobbesian themes that are seen in "Five Characters in Search of an Exit" (based on a short story by Marvin Petal). Here, five characters including an army major, ballerina, clown, hobo and bagpiper, are all in a circular metal room. Serling says "fear, loneliness and the unexplainable walk hand in hand through the shadows." The major wants out and the clown admits to being "governed by human frailty." They work against the element of gravity to get out the top. They cooperate, as Hobbes noted they would, for mutual security and avoidance of fear. The major hooks his sword and pulls himself out. He falls on the snow. He is a toy and is put back in the "Christmas doll drive" bin. So it's not always strive and succeed.

A negative or pessimistic view of human nature is shown in "The Mind and the Matter" where Archibald Beechcroft is a misanthrope.[19] As defined by Fitzgerald Fortune in "A Piano in the House" (by Earl Hamner, Jr.) a misanthrope is "a man who despises people." Beechcroft "battles for survival" in a Malthusian world against a population explosion that includes a commute on a crowded New York City subway. Beechcroft is tired of it all including the "herd" metality of the office and seeks "solitude." He tells his boss it's "people, people, people. If I had my way here's how I'd fix the universe. I'd eliminate the people. I mean cross 'em off, get rid of them, destroy them, decimate them and there'd only be one man left: me."

Beechcroft's asssistant gives him a book that enables him to concentrate on what he wants, mind over matter. He reads the book and decides he wants to concentrate on "getting rid of the people." The book works and he gets rid of the people in the subway and his office. He gets bored with no people, but still insists "I despise people—I loathe them. I've rid myself of the worst scourge there is—the populace." However, there is nothing to do with no people. He decides the only person he can stand is himself, so he creates a world of Beechcroft clones. The subway is full of Beechcrofts, male and female. But they are all misanthropes and he finds this intolerable too. Beechcroft realizes that he can stand other people more than he can stand himself and he's happy to get back to them. One of the clones says "people are pigs" and this is the key phrase because "The Mind and the Matter" has perhaps the most negative view of human nature.

The misanthropy and negative or pessimistic view of human nature expressed here seems like a thread—and Serling's voiceover reinforces this "with all its faults . . . this is the best of all possible worlds." As J. Robert Oppenheimer is supposed to have said "an optimist thinks this is the best of all possible worlds—a pessimist knows it is." And as Hobbes said in the state of nature the life of man is "solitary, poore, nasty, brutish. . . ."[20]

The state of nature is seen in "I Shot an Arrow Into the Air" (based on an idea by Madelon Champion) which showcases the fight for scarce resources and many of the same themes as "The Rip Van Winkle Caper." This show is about a manned spaceship called The Arrow which disappears after take off. The ship crash lands on what appears to be an uninhabited asteroid. Only three of eight survive the crash. The commander tries to keep order but it is the state of nature with scarce resources and only five gallons of water.

The astronauts start fighting over the water. One of the astronauts, Corey, tells the commander that the third man is dead and takes his water. But they find the third man, Pierson, and he's alive. He tries to tell them something with a symbol in the sand. It's a symbol of a cross. Corey takes the captain's gun and tells the captain that there is only enough water for one of them. The captain accuses Corey of killing Pierson.

Corey kills the captain, saying "you brought the chain of command . . ." but it doesn't fit in the state of nature—those rules don't apply. He says "this is a jungle where only the tough animals survive and they don't do it according to the rules" or, as Hobbes says, the war of all against all, *bellum omnium contra omnes*. He has turned into one of those wild and lawless creatures of the Hobbesian state of nature and tells the captain "you were looking for morality in the wrong place." Hobbes says that people are equal and therefore have equality in the hope of obtaining things and "From this equality of ability ariseth equality of hope in the attaining of our ends. And therefore if any two men desire the same thing, which nevertheless they cannot both enjoy, they become enemies; and in the way to their end (which is principally their own conservation, and sometimes their delectation only) endeavour to destroy or subdue one another."[21] When there is only enough water for one it puts them in a state of war with each other.

Corey climbs over the mountains and sees a sign for Reno, Nevada, and realizes they never left Earth. They landed in the desert and the symbol that Pierson drew was a telephone pole. Corey is sorry when he realizes he is on Earth and the rules and laws do apply.

The theme of "Elegy," written by Charles Beaumont, is in keeping with the negative view of human nature and the idea that we can never have peace in the world, or universe, until there are no people.

In "Elegy" three men land on another planet that looks like Earth, but there are two suns so it can't be Earth. The people there don't move. The astronauts go into a Victorian house and encounter a man named Jeremy Wickwire who assures them not to be afraid. Wickwire mentions that most of the Earth was destroyed in a 1985 atomic war (another of Serling's themes) and proposes a toast to peace—explaining that you couldn't have peace on Earth because there are people on Earth, and where there are people there is war. As Hobbes said, belligerence is part of human nature.

The astronauts are on an asteroid that is made to look like Earth. People are stuffed—there are stuffed contestants in a beauty pageant, etc. Wickwire serves the astronauts a drink that kills them—when they ask "why?" he answers "because you are men. And while there are men there can be no peace." What about the fact that Mr. Wickwire is a man? It turns out that Mr. Wickwire is a robot. The theme is that there can only be peace in a place where people don't exist and where robots rule. Perhaps this is why Serling was obsessed with the theme of "automata" or robots in such shows as "I Sing the Body Electric," "Casey at the Bat," "Uncle Simon," "The Brain Center at Whipples," etc.

Hobbes said "life is a race" ("Elements of Law") and man is motivated to compete in the race. If man cannot compete he cannot truly fulfill himself. Man, therefore, must always be striving and competing for something—money, glory, reputation, honors, etc.

In "Escape Clause" Walter Bedeker is a man who takes himself out of the race of life and regrets it. Human nature is such, according to Hobbes, that we need something to strive for—when all our wishes are granted that's when we are truly unhappy.

Bedeker is a hypochondriac preoccupied with sickness and doctors but there is nothing wrong with him. This is his hobby. It's all in his head and his illnesses manufactured, according to the doctor. The focus of his ambition—trying to get a doctor who will tell him he's sick. His wife, Ethel, plays along.

Mr. Bedeker ("Bed" "decker" one who "bedecks the bed") is miserable until a man named Cadwallader appears in his room and makes him a deal—eternal life in return for his soul. Cadwallader is the devil and he'll make Bedeker indestructible.

Bedeker accepts the deal and signs the contract but it has an "escape clause" by which he can furnish his exit if he wants to and get out of the deal. He assures the devil that he won't want to invoke the escape clause.

Bedeker tests the contract—he jumps in front of a subway train and gets run over but emerges without a scratch. He's restless and says "there isn't any excitement." He drinks poison and nothing happens. He's disappointed. He'd rather run the race of life. He decides to jump off the roof of his building. His wife tries to stop him and falls off. He tells the police he killed her so he can get the electric chair.

During the trial Bedeker tries to get capital punishment and asks his lawyer not to defend him. But he gets life in prison without parole—his lawyer congratulates him saying "I knew we could do it."

With the prospect of sitting in a jail cell Bedeker invokes the escape clause and the devil gets his soul. Hobbes said "Life is a race" and evey man must run it—that is human nature, from the *Elements of Law*, Part I, chapter 9: "The comparison of the life of man to a race, though it holdeth not in every point, yet it holdeth so well for this our purpose . . . this race we must suppose to have no other goal . . . but being foremost." Without something to compete for, Bedeker needs to get off the treadmill with the escape clause. Note: this show is similar in theme to "A Nice Place to Visit" with the idea that people are competitive.

"The Self-Improvement of Salvadore Ross" (written by Jerry McNeely based on a short story by Henry Slesar) illustrates that man is competitive and acquisitive. Ross's desire to acquire makes him run the race on the treadmill, but he does not follow the rules of the race. Salvadore Ross is a small time hood who wants to marry an educated woman named Leah Maitland, but her father doesn't approve of him. Sal breaks his hand banging on her door and in the hospital meets a man with a cough. Sal offers to swap the broken hand for the cough. This works and he leaves with a cough.

Sal wants to swap and buy his way to the top. The next swap is youth—he swaps youth for a man's apartment and $1 million. Now he has gray hair, the money and apartment, so he trades with a young man who works in the building—one year for $1000. He does the same with the young man's friends until he's back to the age he was, 26.

When Sal has money he goes back to Leah's house but her father doesn't approve—he says Leah needs someone kind. Just then Leah walks in. She says Sal talks differently and Sal says that he met a guy who went to college and made him a deal "I paid him to help me improve my way of talking." Sal says that he's worked so hard at improving himself that even her father can't object but Mr. Matiland asks if he loves Leah and he replies "I want her." Leah says she'll only marry a man with "compassion." She says she wants someone like her father a "compassionate man" and explains that you can't buy it.

The next scene shows Sal and Leah together and happy—they go to her father's house to talk to him. He is in a wheelchair, he is weak. Sal says he's sorry and promises to be a good husband. Mr. Maitland still refuses. Sal asks for compassion and Mr. Maitland says "compassion? Don't you remember? I sold it to you yesterday" and pulls out a gun and shoots him.

This is the truly Hobbesian man—competitive, acquisitive and lacking in the Rousseauian virtue of compassion which he buys from Leah's father to his detriment. Mr. Maitland is now the Hobbesian man who shoots Sal.

Hobbes said that "life is a race" and people are competitive by nature. If there isn't a race to run people get bored. This is the theme of "Of Late I Think of Cliffordville."[22] William Feathersmith is a "robber baron" and Mr. Hecate is the custodian in the building where Feathersmith works. Feathersmith tells Hecate that he started his rise to the top in Cliffordville, Indiana, and Hecate says he is from there too. Feathersmith looks down on Hecate and says "there the similarity ends." Feathersmith says he has everything—but is "still hungry" and Hecate quotes Alexander the Great: "he cried because he had no more worlds to conquer."

Feathersmith wants to go back to Cliffordville and start all over. Getting it, not having it, was fun. He gets off the elevator and he's in the Twilight Zone, with Devlin's travel agency and a travel agent with horns played by Julie Newmar. The elevator figures prominently here as a symbol of social mobility. Mr. Feathersmith's office is on the top floor.

Ms. Devlin asks Mr. Feathersmith about Cliffordville, if he had fun there. Feathersmith says he had no time for fun—he worked, he "dug, scratch, pushed, drove" and he worked his way to the top. "And now . . . you're bored" says Devlin. At the top there's no place to go so he is bored. But Ms. Devlin offers him time travel and says "the pleasure is not in the possession" but "in the struggle to possess" echoing Hobbes' view that people are competitive by nature and, as Tocqueville said, they are restless too.[23]

Ms. Devlin already has Mr. Feathersmith's soul—he is a businessman who drives people to ruin. But he wants to go back to Cliffordville so he can achieve it all again so she charges him money—all his 36 million dollars. She lets him keep $1412.14. He figures he'll make the money back because he knows where the oil in town is and how to manipulate the stock market. He knows all the inventions. When Ms. Devlin says that she can "smooth the way" for him he says that he wants to work for it—that's the fun.

Ms. Devlin sends Mr. Feathershmith back to Cliffordville, 1910, and when he gets off the train there is a horse drawn carriage, one of Serling's symbols for the bucolic America before the World Wars. He wants to buy 1403 accres of land from the banker, and he buys it for $1 an acre and thinks he's getting a good deal because there's oil on the land—but no way to drill for it yet! The technology isn't yet invented. He goes to mechanics shops and tells them about motors, which haven't been invented yet. They laugh at him and work on their buggies. He tells Ms. Devlin that he wants to go back to 1963 but he has no money for the fare. So as the train is leaving he sells the land to a guy, Mr. Hecate, for $40.

Now Mr. Feathersmith is back in 1963 and he's the custodian and Hecate is the executive—they've switched places, as Serling would say, "the old switcheroo." Now Hecate offers to buy Mr. Feathersmith, the custodian, a watch fob. Mr. Feathersmith thought that it would be easy going back in time and making his fortune again—but, as Serling says, the motto of this story is "quit while you're ahead."

Hobbes said "life is a race" and "The Chaser" (written by Robert Presnell based on a story by John Collier) demonstrates that you always need another race to run and another goal or you stagnate. In "The Chaser" a man named Roger Shackleforth is in love with a woman named Leila who doesn't love him. He is the chaser—he chases Leila because she doesn't like him so she becomes more desirable. He wants to be "shackled" but the proverb "be careful what you wish for" applies to him.

Roger stands on line at a phone booth to talk to Leila and he tells her "I must see you" but when he asks her to say something she tells him to go "jump at the moon."

A man on line for the telephone tells Roger about someone who can help him. Roger goes to the man who is sitting in a big library amidst shelves of books. He is a sorcerer. He asks Roger if he wants money or power—Roger says he wants Leila. The sorcerer, Prof. A Daemon, gives him a love potion. He mentions something about "glove cleaner" but Roger wants the love potion, his cheapest item at one dollar. Roger says if it works he'll "be the happiest man in the world."

Roger goes to Leila's and she agrees to have a drink of champagne with him to get it "over with." He puts the potion in her drink and she is in love with him. He is no longer chasing her, she is chasing him. As the saying goes "when the hunter ceases to hunt he becomes the hunted."

Now the tables are turned—they get married, and Leila is groveling and cloying. This is human nature—when you have achieved or acquired something you need another goal or object to achieve or acquire. The acquisitive human always wants as John D. Rockefeller said "just a little more than what you have." Once you have achieved something you are on to the next thing—as Tocqueville said in "Why the Americans are Restless."

Roger goes back to the prof who now charges him $1000 for "glove cleaner" to get rid of Leila. Roger confesses to him "I am going out of my . . . mind. I can't stand it anymore." The love potion costs one dollar, because everyone who uses it needs the glove cleaner for 1000 dollars. The professor says "it's always the same way—first the stimulant, then the chaser."

In the same way "A Nice Place to Visit" (written by Charles Beaumont) demonstrates the acquisitiveness of man and the "race of life." As De Tocqueville noted Americans are "restless amidst prosperity" and keep chasing their "American Dream." For Hobbes, this was the "race of life" and competitiveness of man. People are bored without competition, which is why capitalism was suited to human nature—it provided incentive for the race.

"A Nice Place to Visit" supports the Hobbesian theme "life is a race" and that humans must always be striving for something because that is man's nature. This story is about a two bit crook Henry "Rocky" Valentine who gets shot during a burglary and killed. He wakes up in Heaven where all of his wishes are given to him. He has a personal valet named "Pip" (played by Sebastian Cabot) who is his "guide" in Heaven.

He asks Pip for money, he gets money. Pip brings Rocky to a beautiful apartment sumptuously furnished with art and antiques. Rocky keeps asking Pip "what's the catch?" A closet full of clothes and he dresses like a dandy. There's a table of delicious food. Rocky shoots Pip when he won't taste the food but the bullet goes right through him.

Rocky realizes the police killed him and infers he is in Heaven. His drawers are filled with money, dancing girls appear at his request. He plays roulette and wins every time. He plays the slot machine and wins. He wonders why they let him in there because he was always a crook.

Rocky and Pip go to the hall of records to see if Rocky did anything that would get him into Heaven. He has a criminal record from when he was a child (ironicallyhe was in a gang called "The Angels"). Pip says "what are you going to do now Mr. Valentine?" He always wins, he always has a contingent of girlfriends. He never has to work for any of it so he gets bored. He never has to earn anything he likes. He plays pool and all the balls go in the pickets—there is no challenge.

Rocky says to Pip "I've been in this dump for a month and I can't stand it anymore" he says "I'm bored—there's no excitement around here." He wants to rob a bank. But it's only fun if he can get caught. Pip says that he can do that if he wants but Rocky says it doesn't count "if it's all set up in advance." He realizes he doesn't belong there and that if he has to stay he's "gonna go nuts." Rocky says "I don't belong in Heaven . . . I want to go to the other place" to which Pip laughs and says "whatever gave you the idea you were in Heaven Mr. Valentine? This IS the other place." Serling's voiceover: "a scared angry little man who never got a break. Now he has everything he's ever wanted— and he's going to have to live with it for eternity in the Twilight Zone." This version of "hell" is based on Hobbesian human nature—that men only thrive with competition and acquisitiveness.

State of Nature—Rousseau

In two episodes, "Two" and "Probe 7 Over and Out," we see an actual depiction of the state of nature which occurs after nuclear war—in "Probe 7" astronaut Adam Cook goes to another planet (Earth) after nuclear war on his planet and in "Two" a man and woman are the lone survivors of nuclear war on Earth. In one the state of nature is presented as a Garden of Eden, and in the other it is presented as a place of war where belligerence rules.

The view of the state of nature in "Two" (written by Montgomery Pittman) demonstrates the Hobbesian version including belligerence and diffidence. The Hobbesian state of nature is a state of war, and "such a war as of every-man against every man." This is the famous "war of all against all" that Hobbes said was the state of nature. We do not see the Garden of Eden described by Rousseau.

In "Probe 7 Over and Out" we see more of the Rousseauian state of nature which is like a Garden of Eden where people are not belligerent and acquisitive. Unlike Hobbes, Rousseau saw the state of nature as a state of peace and tranquility, where people were solitary and idle.[24] Rousseau disagreed with Hobbes that the state of nature was a state of war.[25]

The opening scene in "Two" is a bombed out city after one of "man's battles against himself" and it has been five years since there were any people in the town. It is the state of nature, a place with no government, presumably after a nuclear war.

A lone woman walks through the rubble of the town. She is wearing a uniform with what looks like an atomic logo on the back. A man approaches her and she throws things at him and they start fighting. As Hobbes said, they are "diffident" or fearful of each other and seek to defend themselves. Because they are in a state of nature, which is a state of war, and there is no government every person has a right to everything.

In addition, they fight over the scarce resource of food. There is one can of food and the man knocks the woman out in their struggle for it. He sees newspapers from before the war with headlines like "Evacuate City" and a picture of a debutante in a gas mask.

Because the war is over he doesn't see any reason to fight and offers her food saying where there are no governments or states there is no reason for war. Fighting comes from civilization, not human nature. So even though they start out fighting the man expresses that in the state of nature they do not need to keep fighting. This is a Rousseauian view—that fighting comes from governments and civilization, not from human nature.

The man declares peace saying he doesn't want to fight. They are both diffident and confront each other with guns. The woman sees a gown in the window of a bombed out store. He takes it off the mannequin and gives it to her. She shoots at him when realizing that they were on opposite sides in the war. She puts on the gown and they walk off together, but they still have guns.

In "Two" we see two survivors of a war and they deal with each other in a mostly belligerent and Hobbesian way—armed with guns and fighting for scarce resources. There is practically no dialogue. The woman says only one word: "prokrazny."[26] This is an Hobbesian scenario and they both walk off into the sunset together and not fighting, though each is armed with a gun.

"Probe 7" is Serling's view of the state of nature with the original Garden of Eden as the planet Earth onto which Adam Cook lands when his planet blows up in a nuclear war. When Cook crash lands in his spaceship called "Probe 7" he listens to the radio from his planet and his friend tells him there is a nuclear war about to start and he doesn't know which country will win. He says that they went to war and the entire Eastern Seacoast is obliterated and that Cook should be happy he got out—he's in a sanctuary, not a prison.

Cook emerges from the ship and someone has drawn a planetary map in the sand. The last communication from his planet says "we wiped them out, they wiped us out" and mentions a "500 percent increase in the radioactivity around us." The radioer says "whoever you meet there, however you meet them, I hope it can come without fear. . . ."

Cook sees a woman who calls herself "Norda" who sees his gun and runs out of fear. Cook says "it's not just the language it's the breed—it's our way we ultimately always respond to one another." He tells the radioer "I can give you an observation as to the psychological makeup of man. He is a frightened breed. A very frightened breed. Must be a universal trait must be the case wherever there's life. . . ."

But this story has a decidedly Rousseauian ending—Cook picks up some soil and Norda calls it "Earth." Cook says that's the name of this place. Norda calls herself Eve. Eve goes to pick an apple and offers it to Adam. This is Adam and Even in the Garden of Eden/Earth. Perhaps the message is that the battle has a truce long enough to populate Earth. Or perhaps rationality wins over fear. This scene could be considered more Rousseauian than Hobbesian and is one of the few optimistic scenes in *The Twilight Zone*. In a state of nature with no property, status symbols, swimming pools, mansions or the like there is no need for war or competition—this is the message of "Probe 7."

Nonetheless, both views can be seen as Hobbesian. Hobbes noted that the first law of nature is to seek peace, and the second law is to be willing, when others are, to lay down arms against each other.[27] This agreement to lay down arms is the basis for the social contract or government. Cook and Norda lay down arms, but the "Two" do not, and walk off together but each armed. This leaves open the option of using violence once again.

Even in Serling's actual depictions of war his anti war message comes through and the people involved in the war do not want to fight. "A Quality of Mercy" is set during WW II on August 6, 1945, in the Philippine Islands and is Serling's fantasy of how soldiers might act so as to avoid war in the future. Serling says of the soldiers "they have one more battle to fight." There is a harsh platoon leader, the lieutenant, who wants to "pulverize" the enemy and says he's pretty efficient about "killing Japanese." Serling mocks this character and shows him not as human but as subhuman. He is a stereotype and a caricature of a soldier. The Japanese enemies are hiding in a cave and he wants to route them.

One of the American soldiers says "we'll do some killing for you, but don't ask us to stand up and cheer." When the Lieutenant refers to the Japanese with racial epithets the seargent says "they're men, lieutenant" and the lieutenant says he's "either you've got battle fatigue or you're chicken."

The Lieutenant continues saying "did some body forget to tell you when you fight a war, you fight a war and you kill until you're ordered to stop killing?" And the seargent replies "what's your pleasure, lieutenant? How many men have to die before you're satisfied?" to which the Lieutenant replies "offhand I'd say all of them. No matter who they are or where they are. If they're the enemy, they get it. First day of the war or last day of the war—they get it."

The Lieutenant's binoculars fall and all of a sudden he's Japanese. Now *he's* afraid. Americans are shooting at *him*. Now the Americans are in the cave and he is speaking to a Japanese seargent. There is a brutal Japanese Captain, the equivalent of the American Lieutenant, who wants to go into the cave after the Americans. Now the Lieutenant wants to let the wounded Americans surrender, or just leave them there. The Japanese Captain accuses him of inappropriate compassion and says "we have to destroy them. They are Americans. They are enemies . . . they are the enem . . ." and the Lieutenant says "but they are men." The Captain compares them to ants and says "this is war and in war you kill . . . until you are ordered to stop killing." The Lieutenant asks "how many must die before (you are) satisfied?" and the Captain replies "offhand . . . I would say all of them. I don't care where they are or who they are. If they are the enemy they are to be destroyed. First day of the war, last day of the war, we destroy them."

The Lieutenant turns back into an American. The soldiers are ready to go into the cave for the Japanese when the United States drops the atomic bomb in Japan. They want the Americans to pull back. Now the Lieutenant sees that he's not that keen to kill people. He expresses the hope that there will not be any more wars.

The idea of compassion in war is a theme of "No Time Like the Past," where Paul Driscoll goes back in time with a time machine to the day the atom bomb is dropped on Hiroshima. He tries to warn the Japanese police of Hiroshima to evacuate the city because a "new kind" of bomb is going to be dropped. But even though the policeman doesn't believe him he is going to give him a chance to explain and won't shoot him, so he can tell the Americans that "the face of the enemy is not devoid of some compassion." Driscoll says that the same could be said of him—that he tried to warn the people of Hiroshima. The Japanese policeman looks at a picture of his family, hears a plane outside—the lone plane Driscoll said would carry the bomb—and his office blows up.

The anti war message of compassion for the enemy in war stands in contrast to the Hobbesian message, but it is Serling's anti war fantasy. And even Hobbes realized that out of self interest—not compassion for their enemy—people would lay down arms and seek peace.

To Serve Man

If Hobbes' view of human nature was based on a belief in the acquisitive and diffident nature of man then based on many examples from *The Twilight Zone* Serling demonstrates a pessimistic or negative view of human nature including the important Hobbesian elements of fear, greed, glory and belligerence.

Fear is a theme so common in Serling's *Twilight Zone* stories that it may be said to be a leitmotif threaded through stories including "The Fear," "Nervous Man," "Monsters Are Due on Maple Street," etc. These stories demonstrate Serling's belief that humans fear not only aliens but mainly themselves and each other. Time and time again we see repeated the theme that fear keeps us from universal peace ("The Gift") and from trusting others ("To Serve Man"). Fear makes us distrustful of our neighbors ("Monsters"). Fear keeps us from having the kind of harmonious society that Serling may have fantasized about.

If acquisitiveness is important to the Hobbesian view of human nature it is also a key element in many of Serling's *Twilight Zones* including "Rip Van Winkle," "Uncle Simon," "The Masks," which all demonstrate that greed is a great human motivator that Serling looks down on. It cannot be denied that Serling's characters are fearful and belligerent even in the state of nature where there is no society to influence them.

Hobbes, an empirical social scientist, accepted human nature as it was. But Serling, a fantasist, didn't, preferring instead to keep an idealized or romanticized view of what it should or could be. How else to explain Serling's need for retribution to the greedy in such episodes as "Rip Van Winkle," "The Masks," "Uncle Simon"? In Hobbes's philosophy acquisitiveness is not punished because it is value neutral.

Hobbes said that life in the state of nature during a time without government is "solitary, poore, nasty, brutish. . . ." This raises the issue of Serling's "nasty" twists and turns in his stories. For Serling, humans struggle and life is bleak—very rarely do you hit the jackpot and even if you do it's a sinister bargain ("The Fever," "Escape Clause," "A Nice Place to Visit").

This theme is seen again and again in *The Twilight Zone* in shows including "Escape Clause," "Execution," "Time Enough at Last," "To Serve Man,"

"A Stop at Willoughby," "A Most Unusual Camera," "The Rip Van Winkle Caper," "The Silence," "The Man in the Bottle." In each story there is a nasty ending that comes as a trick or surprise—but not as a trick to Serling. Serling's belief in the "nasty and brutish" side of human nature existed not only in the state of nature but also in society and betrays a pessimistic view of human nature.

The pessimistic view of human nature is superimposed onto aliens who become superhuman yet take on many negative traits of humans including greed and deviousness. Examples include "To Serve Man" where the Kanamits pretend to be benefactors but turn out to be carnivorous with a taste for Earthlings. Just as people turn on each other, aliens turn on Earthlings. This theme is seen perhaps most dramatically in "Monsters on Maple St." where aliens harness human nature and "man's inhumanity to man" against them. The theme is also seen in "Hocus Pocus and Frisby" where sinister aliens pretend to be humans in order to enslave humans.

"People Are Alike All Over" (based on a short story by Paul Fairman) demonstrates the same theme of pessimism. Aliens put humans in cages after luring them into a false sense of security. The story is unremarkable until the last scene.

In "People Are Alike" two astronauts—Sam Conrad and Warren Marcusson—are going to Mars. Sam is afraid, not reassured, by Marcusson's theory that "people are the same all over." They crash land and only Sam survives. But he finds the Martians look like people and are friendly.

Sam doesn't want to leave the spaceship because "people are alike all over." Marcusson doesn't make it out of the ship because Sam won't open the door. The door opens. Sam is armed with a gun. But the people outside are friendly.

The Martian takes Sam's gun and throws it away. The bait they use is an attractive lady named Teenya. They take Sam to a house they built for him. "We assume this is the way you people live." They read Sam's mind to find out how to build an Earth house which looks like a 1950s style ranch house. Teenya looks sad as the Martians leave Sam in the house.

Sam notices something strange about the house—the doors won't open. The Martians have caged him. The wall opens and there are bars like a jail or a cage at the zoo and the Martians are looking at him from the other side of the bars. The sign outside says "Earth creature in his native habitat."

Sam realizes he is in an interplanetary zoo and says "Marcusson—you were right. You were right. People are alike. People are alike everywhere."

"To Serve Man" (based on a short story by Damon Knight) is one of the shows that people remember from *The Twilight Zone*. If you remember only one show it is likely to be this one, or "Time Enough at Last." "To Serve Man" has a similar theme to "People Are Alike" and a similarly ironic twist that demonstrates the same pessimism.

The story of "To Serve Man" is this: aliens land on Earth and help humans. The Secretary General of the United Nations proclaims that creatures from outer space, the Kanamits, have come to Earth. One of the Kanamits, 9 ft. tall, addresses the UN. He greets the people of the Earth in peace and friendship and has honorable intentions. A man named Mr. Chambers narrates. He says the listeners may have questions for the Kanamits and question their intentions because humans "as a race we are unaccustomed to charity. Brutality is a far more universal language to us than an expression of friendship from outer space."

The Kanamits want to help people of Earth with new atomic power sources, new agricultural methods, and other improvements. The Soviet representative to the UN assumes an ulterior motive, but the Kanamit says he will demonstrate how to end famine on earth and to let these improvements demonstrate his motives. The Kanamit also says he will introduce a missile shield or a "force field in which you may cloak each nation with an invisible wall absolutely impenetrable by bombs, missiles, or anything else."[28] The Kanamit asks the people to trust them.

The Kanamit leaves a book at the UN and the White House feels if the decoders can decipher the book they will know the real motives of the Kanamits. But Chambers says "they've done alright by us so far." De-coding specialists for the U.S. government (including Mr. Chambers, the narrator) try to crack the Kanamit language to decipher their real motives. But they are "500 times more intelligent than we are." One of the generals calls their antics "parlor tricks" i.e., the new approach to nitrate use to enrich the soil. Mr. Chambers says that with the Kanamits help there will be "no more wars, or diseases or famines" and the Earth will be a "Garden of Eden."[29] The Colonels are more realistic and, while they admire Chambers' optimism, tell him to keep trying to decipher the book. Mr. Chambers' assistant deciphers the book's title: *To Serve Man*.

Pretty soon armies and navies are practically disbanded because the missile shield ends war. The Earth can grow more food to end famines. The Kanamit's advice improves the Earth. Tourists are traveling from Earth to the Kanamits' planet. One of the decoders comments that there is no work for them because "we are not reading about hydrogen bomb or war scares, or insurrections anymore."

Mr. Chambers reveals to his assistant, the decoder, that he is going to the Kanamits' planet. The decoder says she is still trying to decipher the Kanamit book *To Serve Man*. As Mr. Chambers is boarding the ship to the Kanamits' planet the decoder tells him not to get on the ship because *To Serve Man* is a cookbook. Chambers is hauled up the stairs into the ship—it takes off, and Chambers is seen in a room on the ship where the Kanamit offers him food saying "we wouldn't want you to lose weight." Serling's voiceover: man has gone from "being the ruler of a planet to an ingredient in someone's soup." This is the flip side of "The Gift," where people should have trusted the alien.

Another twist of a pessimistic variety comes in the classic "Time Enough at last" (based on a short story by Lynn Venable) about a bookish bank clerk named Henry Bemis. He wears thick glasses and doesn't have his mind on his work. He spends most of his time reading the classics, including Dickens, in the bank vault.

Rod Serling introduces "Time Enough at Last" by saying Bemis will have "a world to himself, without anyone." This theme of a world without people is also seen in "Elegy" and "Mind and the Matter." Because people make war and are greedy and belligerent wouldn't the world would be a beautiful place without them?

One lunch time when Mr. Bemis goes into the bank vault to read there is an atomic explosion and everything is annihilated. Bemis emerges from the vault to a nuclear terrain in which there are no people.

Mr. Bemis doesn't like to be alone. He finds a gun and is about to kill himself until he comes across the wreckage of a library and sees there are books by Dickens, Shelley, Shakespeare, etc. He makes a reading list, stacks the books and sits down on the steps of the library to read, which he now has time to do. As he reaches for a book his glasses fall and break. We see what he sees—everything blurry. Now he has books, books everywhere and can't read. He says "that's not fair. That's not fair at all." Now Mr. Bemis is "just a fragment of what man has deeded himself."

The twist in "Time Enough at Last" is like the one in "Escape Clause"—the "nasty and brutish" Hobbesian part always comes out. No matter how good a bargain or deal you seem to have swung—won the slot machine, been granted your wish—it backfires and ensnares you in a prison that is of your own making. As Larry Blyden says in "A Nice Place to Visit," "I want to go to the other place" to which Sebastian Cabot replies "this is the other place."

Serling is an apologetic Hobbesian. He has a negative view of human nature like Hobbes for which he feels he needs to apologize and create scenarios more optimistic. This is what he does in "Probe 7" and it is also what he does in "Where is Everybody?" which demonstrates his belief in man as a social creature or, as Aristotle said "zoon politikon."

"Where is Everybody?" is about an experiment on how astronauts will react to isolation. The opening scene is the Garden of Eden—a single man walking through a forest with mist around. He encounters an empty café where the juke box is playing and food is cooking indicating that people had been there recently.

He leaves the café and walks to an empty town. He tries to call "O" on a pay phone and gets an automated recording. He walks around and everywhere sees signs that people were there—a half smoked cigar, shaving equipment, even in the jail. He asks "where is everybody?"

He walks into a drug store and makes himself a sundae. He feels he is in a nightmare and quotes Ebenezer Scrooge that his dream is "an undigested bit of beef." He says he wants to "wake up" or "at least . . . find somebody to talk to."

He sees a book at the drugstore "The Last Man on Earth." Now it is dark. He is alone. He remembers he is in the Air Force. He starts to say "help me." Just then we see he is being watched on a TV by a group of men on a closed circuit TV. They say "release the subject." He is the subject of an experiment to see how he would react to being alone in space. But he had delusions after being locked in a box. When asked about his experience he says he was at "a place I don't want to go again . . . a town without people, without anybody."

The Air Force doctor says "we can feed the stomach with concentrates, we can supply microfilm . . . we can pump oxygen in . . . but there's one thing we can't simulate that's a very basic need—man's hunger for companionship, the barrier of loneliness." He is told "next time you'll really be alone." He looks up at the moon. Serling's voiceover says "up there is an enemy known as isolation."

"Where is Everybody?" suggests Serling's belief that man cannot survive without other people—a theme also seen in "The Mind and the Matter" and "The Lonely" and that even though people are belligerent and quarrelsome ("Monsters on Maple St.") they need other people.

Also from season one the theme of "The Lonely" is that competitive and belligerent people need other people. This is a story about a man, James A. Corry, banished to an asteroid who lives in isolation in an interplanetary jail. He is a "convicted criminal . . . in solitary confinement" and he is dependent on people from Earth to bring him food and supplies.[30]

Corry keeps a diary and we see him in his fourth year of isolation. He is starting to get depressed when the ship from Earth lands to bring him supplies. Corry wants the crew to stay and play cards but the commander says they can only stay for 15 minutes. Corry implores them to stay and play chess. Every morning when he gets up he tells himself "this is my last day of sanity. I can't stand this loneliness one more day."

Corry feels like a caged animal. Commander Allenby explains that he can't give Corry a pardon, but he can bring him whatever might help him to "fight loneliness." One such thing is a robot in the shape of a woman. Her name is Alicia and she is just like a real person. At first Corry doesn't want her there because she's fake. She is a reminder to him that he's "so lonely (he's) about to lose his mind" until he sees her crying and then he apologizes. They play checkers. He is not lonely anymore. He teaches her the constellations and they gaze at the stars.

Allenby's ship comes back and he tells Corry that he has "good news." Corry has received a pardon. They ask Corry to get ready to go to Earth immediately, but they only have room for 15 pounds of stuff so they can't take Alicia. Corry wants to take her saying "she kept me alive." He now has to decide between leaving or staying with Alicia on the asteroid. Allenby decides for him. He takes his gun and shoots Alicia. Her face becomes a robot's face full of wires. Allenby explains "all you're leaving behind is loneliness."

"The Lonely" reinforces Serling's belief that man is a social animal and that even though he is often belligerent and competitive he is only suited to exist in society. This is an ancient view expressed by Plato and Aristotle and decidedly in Hobbesian. Hobbes did not see society as natural but as a contract, artificial and not the product of nature. People do not want to be with each other and only agree to society or government to keep peace among them out of self interest. Perhaps Corry's need for Alicia is out of self interest but perhaps it isn't, this is the Rousseauian part of Serling, the part that sees man as compassionate and social contrary to his more negative portrayals.

However upbeat the message of "The Lonely," Serling agrees with Hobbes and emphasizes that people are distrustful of each other which is the theme of "Will the Real Martian Please Stand Up?" where it is on display.

In "Martian" a UFO lands in a snowy pond in Hooks Landing and two state troopers see footprints coming out of the pond leading to a diner in the woods where a bus is parked. The troopers go into the diner where the people from the bus are taking refuge. The roads are blocked because of the snow and the passengers marooned. There is a young couple, a businessman, a single woman, an older couple and a strange looking older man who the businessman doesn't remember on the bus. The bus driver had six people on the bus but there are seven people at the diner. One of them didn't get off the bus.

One person in the diner is from the UFO and the passengers begin to suspect each other. The single woman suggests eliminating the couple—but the woman starts to suspect the young man. The couples start suspecting each other. The older man says to his wife "I'll thank you to stop looking at me as if I've just put on this face as part of a costume." The strange single man says "she don't know who he is, he don't know who she is, we don't know who she is, and this lemon sucker here (pointing to businessman) he's the most suspicious of the bunch."

The state trooper asks the strange man who won the world series—"You didn't figure us Martians" would know about baseball, but he knows. The trooper asks the single woman for identification. Her name is Ethel McConnell, the bus driver vouches for her saying "she's the only one I noticed." The businessman is getting annoyed by all the questioning and just then the juke box goes on by itself. Everyone looks at everyone else suspiciously. The lights go out. The trooper wants to confine the Martian in the diner, but they don't know who that is. The sugar bowls break, the pay phone rings—it's the county engineer saying that the bridge is ok. They pay for their food and leave the diner.

The people get back on the bus. The businessman walks back to the diner and tells the proprietor that the bridge collapsed, no one got out except him. The proprietor says to the businessman "but you're not even wet." The businessman replies "wet. What's wet?" The businessman reveals he has three arms and is the Martian. The proprietor reveals a third eye and says he's from Venus.

The theme of "Martian" is that distrust is an essential part of human nature and it takes very little to bring it out. Governments and aliens, as the Martians and Venusians (and even the aliens in "The Monsters Are Due on Maple St."), use the distrust to their advantage. An Hobbesian view, it seems—as is the view in "I Dream of Genie" where vanity, greed and thirst for power are on display as basic aspects of human nature.

In "I Dream of Genie," written by John Furia, Jr., a man named George P. Hanley (with a dog named Attila) finds a bottle out of which comes a genie who gives three wishes. George first wishes to be married to a famous and glamorous actress. He soon tires of this. His next wish is for money, which he donates to his alma mater. The alma mater returns it saying it is too ostentatious. Finally, George asks for power and becomes President of the United States. He likes this until he must make decisions about war and peace. At this point he wishes to be a genie so he can grant others' wishes.

For Serling, glory can be seen as noble but often becoming the vice of pride or vanity, (Rousseau's *amour-propre* where "whoever sang or danced best" got the most attention) but is not punished as much as greed. Greed seems to be Serling's "Achilles' heel" when it comes to vice and virtue and the greedy (Barbara, the crooks in "Rip Van Winkle," the family in "Masks") are suitably punished in the most "zonish" ways. Again, Serling is an apologetic Hobbesian—for Hobbes humans are acquisitive, but for Serling humans are greedy and they must be punished for their greed.

Notes

1. "Submitted for Your Approval," *American Masters*, PBS TV show produced and directed by Susan Lacy and written by Thomas Wagner and John Goff, 1995.

2. See Isaac Kramnick and "Equal Opportunity and The Race of Life" *Dissent*, Vol. 28, 1981 and Alexis De Tocqueville, *Democracy in America*, Introduction by

Thomas Bender, Modern Library (NY:1981) p. 431, also Hobbes, *Elements of Law*, Part I, ch. 9.

3. Alexis De Tocqueville, *Democracy in America*, "Why the Americans are so Restless in the midst of their prosperity" Vol II, Book 2.

4. Ibid., see Tocqueville on ambition and the role of chance in the American Dream.

5. Hobbes says of the state of nature "So that in the nature of man, we find three principal causes of quarrel. First, competition; secondly, diffidence; thirdly, glory. The first maketh men invade for gain; the second, for safety; and the third, for reputation. The first use violence, to make themselves masters of other men's persons, wives, children, and cattle; the second, to defend them; the third, for trifles, as a word, a smile, a different opinion, and any other sign of undervalue, either direct in their persons or by reflection in their kindred, their friends, their nation, their profession, or their name.

Hereby it is manifest that during the time men live without a common power to keep them all in awe, they are in that condition which is called war; and such a war as is of every man against every man. For war consisteth not in battle only, or the act of fighting, but in a tract of time, wherein the will to contend by battle is sufficiently known: and therefore the notion of time is to be considered in the nature of war, as it is in the nature of weather. For as the nature of foul weather lieth not in a shower or two of rain, but in an inclination thereto of many days together: so the nature of war consisteth not in actual fighting, but in the known disposition thereto during all the time there is no assurance to the contrary. All other time is peace.

Whatsoever therefore is consequent to a time of war, where every man is enemy to every man, the same consequent to the time wherein men live without other security than what their own strength and their own invention shall furnish them withal. In such condition there is no place for industry, because the fruit thereof is uncertain: and consequently no culture of the earth; no navigation, nor use of the commodities that may be imported by sea; no commodious building; no instruments of moving and removing such things as require much force; no knowledge of the face of the earth; no account of time; no arts; no letters; no society; and which is worst of all, continual fear, and danger of violent death; and the life of man, solitary, poor, nasty, brutish, and short" *Leviathan*, ch. 13

6. Plato has a theory of recollection—that all knowledge is a recollection, Plato's *Republic*.

7. Thanks to Simona Fordyce for identifying this theme.

8. This is also used in "Nervous Man in a Four Dollar Room" and "Last Night of a Jockey," not so dramatically.

9. According to Carol Serling "Rod absolutely loved Dickens, and he loved that story" meaning *A Christmas Carol*, quoted in "Marley is Dead, Killed in a Nuclear War" by Thomas Vinciguerra, *NY Times*, Dec 20, 2007, p. E12

10. His wife is played by the same actress in "The Fever" which is also about greed and compulsion.

11. Note: the device of the mesh wire from "Nick of Time" appears again as if the genie is weaving a web.

12. Flora makes fun of bandstand concerts, which Serling inserts into his "homey" stories about main streets and home towns—her derision of them convinces us that she really only cares about money.

13. The themes of fascism, and "big v. small" are prominent Serling themes. The statue of Craig being pulled down looks exactly like the statue of Saddam Hussein being pulled down in Iraq in 2003.

14. Hobbes, Thomas, *Leviathan*, ch. 13

15. Serling used the Scrooge theme again in "Carol for Another Christmas" in 1964 where "three spirits work their reformational magic." "Marley is Dead, Killed in a Nuclear War" by Thomas Vinciguerra, *NY Times*, Dec 20, 2007.

16. See Isaac Kramnick, "Equal Opportunity and The Race of Life" *Dissent*, vol. 28, 1981.

17. Hobbes, *Leviathan*, ch. 13.

18. References to Ithaca, New York, among other upstate New York cities are common in *The Twilight Zone* because of the proximity to Serling's hometown of Binghamton. The setting of "Mirror Image" may be the Ithaca bus station.

19. Serling likes to repeat names. The name Beechcroft is also used in "Changing of the Guard." The name Finchley is similarly used in "A Thing About Machines" and "Mr. Finchley versus the Bomb" another story written for *The Kaiser Aluminum Hour*.

20. Hobbes, *Leviathan*, ch. 13.

21. Hobbes, *Leviathan* ch. 13.

22. Written by Serling, based on a short story "Blind Alley" by Malcolm Jameson.

23. In *Democracy in America* De Tocqueville characterizes the American Dream of social mobility and American restlessness as a "bootless chase" Book II, chapter XIII. "Why the Americans are so restless in the midst of their prosperity": "It is strange to see with what feverish ardor the Americans pursue their own welfare" and that equal conditions have "swept away the privileges of some of their fellow creatures . . . which stood in their way, but they have opened the door to universal competition."

24. "Hobbes contends that man is naturally intrepid, and is intent only upon attacking and fighting. Another illustrious philosopher holds the opposite, and Cumberland and Puffendorf also affirm that nothing is more timid and fearful than man in the state of nature; that he is always in a tremble, and ready to fly at the least noise or the slightest movement. This may be true of things he does not know; and I do not doubt his being terrified by every novelty that presents itself, when he neither knows the physical good or evil he may expect from it, nor can make a comparison between his own strength and the dangers he is about to encounter. Such circumstances, however, rarely occur in a state of nature, in which all things proceed in a uniform manner, and the face of the earth is not subject to those sudden and continual changes which arise from the passions and caprices of bodies of men living together." Rousseau, *Discourse on Origin of Inequality*.

25. See Rousseau, *Discourse on the Origin of Inequality*. Rousseau says "let us not conclude, with Hobbes, that because man has no idea of goodness, he must be naturally wicked . . ." and that Hobbes has a "false sense" of human nature, *Social Contract and Discourses*, translated by GDH Cole, Everyman's Library (Dent: 1973) p. 65.

26. "Prokrazny" sounds Russian and is perhaps meant to indicate that the war was between America and the USSR, considering that it was produced during the height of the "Cold War" September, 1961 just after the Bay of Pigs.

27. "Whensoever a man transferreth his right, or renounceth it, it is either in consideration of some right reciprocally transferred to himself, or for some other good he hopeth for thereby. For it is a voluntary act: and of the voluntary acts of every man, the object is some good to himself. The first branch of which rule containeth the first and fundamental law of nature, which is: to seek peace and follow it. The second, the sum of the right of nature, which is: by all means we can to defend ourselves.

From this fundamental law of nature, by which men are commanded to endeavour peace, is derived this second law: that a man be willing, when others are so too, as far forth as for peace and defence of himself he shall think it necessary, to lay down this right to all things; and be contented with so much liberty against other men as he would allow other men against himself. For as long as every man holdeth this right, of doing anything he liketh; so long are all men in the condition of war. But if other men will not lay down their right, as well as he, then there is no reason for anyone to divest himself of his: Whensoever a man transferreth his right, or renounceth it, it is either in consideration of some right reciprocally transferred to himself, or for some other good he hopeth for thereby. For it is a voluntary act: and of the voluntary acts of every man, the object is some good to himself." Hobbes, *Leviathan*, ch. 14.

28. This anticipates SDI or the "Star Wars" missile shield popularized by Ronald Reagan.

29. The Garden of Eden state that Serling fantasizes about is mentioned.

30. One wonders if Serling thinks of this as against the "cruel and unusual punishment" of the Eighth Amendment. Corry is on an asteroid 9 million miles from Earth, "a man dying of loneliness."

2

The Individual and the State

THE INDIVIDUAL'S RELATION TO THE STATE is a main and important theme of Serling in *The Twilight Zone*. Many important shows consider this theme along with the theme of political power and the nature of the state. Serling generally sees the state as an imposing force that wields power over the individual ("The Obsolete Man," "Eye of the Beholder") that is omniscient and oppressive. The state has the power to execute and to manipulate, to mould and punish, but does Serling ever see the state as an institution of democratic governance?

Freedom and Conformity

In a June 1967 interview with the *Los Angeles Times*, Serling said, "I want all men to have freedom, and I'm not opposed to picking up a cudgel, or a rifle, to help supply or maintain that freedom," but also said, in "No Time Like the Past," "patriotism doesn't have to come with pain." This is the line he straddled—patriot and pacifist, with a strong belief in the importance of individual rights. Like Hobbes, Serling rejects the idea of a higher truth or one "right" way to live—instead focusing on the pursuit of happiness. In ch. xxi of *Leviathan* Hobbes describes freedom as the "absence of opposition" to external impediments of motion. This theme comes out most forcefully in such shows as "The Obsolete Man" and "The Eye of the Beholder" where individual freedom is put against the majesty and power of the state. This is Serling's fear—that the state will subvert freedom—and he reminds us that "any state . . . that fails to recognize the worth, the dignity, the rights of man—that state is obsolete."

When asked by Mike Wallace in a 1959 interview if he was a conformist because of television censorship, Serling replied that he was not a conformist but, in writing *The Twilight Zone*, "acting the role of a tired non-conformist."[1] Serling wanted to write about important issues such as conformity in society and he could probably get around the censors more easily if he wrote "science fiction." He refused to admit to Wallace that he gave in to censorship about these issues—or he admitted it reluctantly.

Alexis de Tocqueville talked about the dangers of conformity and monotonous equality in *Democracy in America* where he said "none but attentive and clear-sighted men perceive the perils with which equality threatens us, and they commonly avoid pointing them out" and stated that Americans ". . . call for equality in freedom; and if they cannot obtain that, they still call for equality in slavery."[2] De Tocqueville thought that the "Tyranny of the Majority" would exert a force over society in which individuals would be forced into conformity of thought, word and action ("thought is an invisible and subtle power . . .") and said: "In America the majority raises formidable barriers around the liberty of opinion" and "I know of no country in which there is so little independence of mind and real freedom of discussion as in America."[3]

"Mirror Image" in the first season introduces the idea of conformity, and presents the idea that each of us has a double, perhaps alluding to the theme of consumer society where everybody looks like, or wants to look like, everybody else.

Millicent Barnes is sitting in the bus depot waiting for a bus to Cortland. She asks the ticket seller when the bus is going to arrive and he says she's already asked before—but she hasn't. She sees a suitcase that looks exactly like hers. We are told by Serling that she is "not a very imaginative type." She asks about the bag near the ticket seller that looks like hers and he tells her it is hers—but she says she didn't check her bag.

Millicent goes to the bathroom. She checks her face—it's still her. The bathroom attendant says she was just there, but she wasn't. Now she looks in the mirror and sees a reflection of herself sitting in the bus station. Why is she going to Cortland? Does she have a job interview? She is a private secretary who quit her job and got a job in a city in upstate New York where she is headed.

A man, Paul Grinstead from Binghamton, befriends Millicent and sees she's acting strangely. The bus arrives and she sees herself sitting on it. She faints. The man, Paul Grinstead, waits with her and she wonders about "parallel worlds that exist side by side" in which we have doubles or "counterparts."

Paul Grinstead calls the police and they come and take her—but then he sees a man running away with his briefcase—he chases him and sees that it's himself.

What is Serling trying to tell us in "Mirror Image"? Perhaps he is alluding to the day that society becomes so conformist and monotonous everyone thinks alike and even looks alike. Perhaps the "mirror image" symbolizes what Tocqueville meant when he alluded to the Tyranny of the Majority or to the sameness of communism or a bureaucratic state that applauds conformity. Millicent Barnes is confused by "delusions" but perhaps it's just the brainwashing that goes on in bourgeois consumer society that reinforces the sameness and monotony that Tocqueville spoke of. There is a big sign in the bus station that says "check your baggage here"—maybe baggage is symbolic for thoughts and ideas maybe it means check your thoughts so that you won't think independently.

"The Obsolete Man" is a case in point in which the majesty and power of the state is used to "eliminate" people who are "obsolete" as judged by the state. Here the individual is pitted against the state—a fascist state which is not, as in Hobbes, meant to protect the rights of the individual but to take them away, to abuse and manipulate individuals. Serling is disturbed by giving the state power—if you've given it the power to do good you've also given it the power to do bad. This is Tocqueville gone awry—not his "soft despotism" which would be like a beneficial dictator—but the full power of the fascist state set at odds with the individual and his rights.

In "Obsolete Man" we see a man seated at a long table. In back of him is a man at a high podium. They represent the state. They say "Wordsworth, Romney. Obsolescence." The state is seen as an impersonal and imposing entity with dictatorial power that is devoted to "the destruction of human freedom" Romney Wordsworth "is a citizen of the state but will soon have to be eliminated." The man at the high podium, the Chancellor, calls out "Wordsworth, Romney. Field investigation finding—obsolescence."

The state has found Mr. Wordsworth to be obsolete. What does this mean? It means that because he is a librarian (with Burgess Meredith playing much the same role as in "Time Enough at Last") and because the state is now burning books, he is obsolete.

The Chancellor asks him if he understands the implications of the charge of obsolescence. He says "I am a librarian . . . If 'you people' choose to call that obsolete." The Chancellor takes exception to the term "you people" for the state and asks Wordsworth if he makes reference to the state. Wordsworth says he refers to the state. The Chancellor likes to think of the state as imposing, not as a collection of people—but we'll see that he is wrong. The state is embodied in one leader, but that leader is a person.

Wordsworth says of the importance of the individual "I'm a human being— I exist, if I speak one thought aloud that thought lives. . . ." The Chanceller says "you have no strength at all" and the individual's ideas, poetry, literature amount to nothing—they are "delusions." They are "an opiate to make you think you have strength" and "the state has no use for your kind."

"The Board" by which we understand the state considers Wordsworth obsolete and will "liquidate" him in 48 hours. He can choose the method— "pills, gas, electrocution." Wordsworth requests an assassin to whom he'll tell the method of liquidation. He also requests an audience and the Chancellor explains that the state televises executions because it's educational.

Wordsworth is in his room filled with books, the Chancellor is there too. He explains that he came to show that "the state has no fears—none at all." Wordsworth says that the state must be pretty weak if it has to prove that it's not afraid of a librarian. Usually the state dictates and individuals usually "follow and obey." The Chancellor says to Wordsworth "we'll see then which is the stronger, the state or the librarian." The Chancellor explains the state can put 1300 people to death "in less than 6 hours." The state must get rid of the "undesirables" or they could overthow the state. Individuals who "could perform no useful function for the state" are liquidated by the state.

There is a closed circuit TV camera in the room that the assassins have put there. Wordsworth explains that a bomb is going off in his room and they are locked in. Wordsworth reads the Bible—a crime—and the Chancellor starts to sweat and bang on the door. Now Wordsworth is cool. The Chancellor says "you're insane if you think they'll let me stay here." Now he refers to the state as "they" Wordsworth asks the Chancellor to face the camera to "let the whole country see the strength of the state, the resilience of the state, the courage of the state." He is the symbol of authority versus an "insignificant librarian" says Wordsworth and "there is precious little to distinguish us."

At midnight the Chancellor tries to break out. Wordsworth lets him out just before the room blows up. But now he has shown himself to be obsolete and up for liquidation. A chorus chants "obsolete" closing in on the Chancellor. They chase him and drag him on the table. Serling's voiceover: "any state, any entity, any ideology that fails to recognize the worth, the dignity the rights of man—that state is obsolete."

Serling focuses on the brutality of the state and the abuse of its power at the expense of the individual. Yet, as the American founders knew, the state is made up of people. The Chancellor can be liquidated when he is proven to be more timid than the librarian—he is a person even though "the state" is shown to be monolithic and all powerful.

John Locke used the image of the state as a parental figure that controls people. Just as the parents dominate in the household and enforce rules the state dominates and enforces the rules of society. The state is the enforcer of rules and according to Locke this is good—because "where there is no law there is no freedom" and "that ill deserves the name of confinement which hedges us in only from bogs and precipices. So that, however it may be mistaken, the end of law is not to abolish or restrain, but to preserve and enlarge freedom."[4] Aristotle agrees saying, in *The Politics*, man "if he be isolated from law and justice he is the worst of all."

But Locke was against monarchy, the idea of the state having monolithic power to rule, or power with no limits being placed in the state. The whole idea of Locke is that government by the people is based on their consent—the social contract creates obligations on both the state and the people. The state's power can be withdrawn by their consent, particularly if there is tyranny defined as government's abuse of power or a ruler or government with "a long train of abuses." The Lockean state must protect the people and put limits on its power in return for consent. If the state fails to protect, or limit its power the people can withdraw their consent. This is the Lockean right of revolution.

The idea that government or the state is at odds with the people is neither Lockean nor Hobbesian. Hobbes saw the state as authoritarian, and with more power than Locke's, but Hobbes discusses the importance of the individual and individual freedom. The state can abridge freedom only to keep order—so that there can be peace. But to abridge freedom is, according to Locke and Hobbes, to protect freedom for "that ill deserves the name of confinement which hedges us in only from the bogs and precipices."[5] For Hobbes the law is a hedge that keeps the traveler in his way "For the use of Lawes (which are but Rules Authorised) is not to bind the People from all Voluntary actions; but to direct and keep them in such a motion, as not to hurt themselves . . . as Hedges are set, not to stop Travellers, but to keep them in the way."[6]

Thus, for both Hobbes and Locke the liberal democratic state hedges in the individual only to protect his rights and freedom, not to trample on them. The individual and civil liberties are very important in the philosophies of both. Hobbes chapter I is "Of Man" not "Of the state." Man creates the state, not vice versa. For Hobbes, the state, or contract cannot be broken but it doesn't matter—the state created by individuals will not hurt them because of every act the Sovereign does it is of some benefit for the individuals.[7] Because the individuals are the authors of everything the Sovereign does, and because they only act in their own interest, the Sovereign won't act against the individual's interests.

Clearly, the state in "The Obsolete Man" is neither the Lockean nor the Hobbesian liberal state, but a tyranny. Both Hobbes and Locke recognized the dangers of tyranny and included protections in their liberal states including rights for the individual, consent of the governed, and limits on the state's power.

Serling, as a liberal, is in agreement with the Lockean and Hobbesian concept of the state as a neutral player that will settle disputes of individuals based on the rule of law. Therefore, Serling's idea of the worst state—that in "The Obsolete Man" and other shows—is also Hobbes's and Locke's and Aristotle's idea of the worst state, tyranny.

Tyranny of the individual by the state is the theme in "The Eye of the Beholder." In this show we see a woman, Janet Tyler, in a hospital bed with her
head bandaged. It is not clear how she can even breathe through the bandages
but this is done for effect. Something is wrong with Miss Tyler's face. She is
deformed. People scream when they look at her. We cannot see the nurses or
the doctors, the show is shot in shadows.

The nurses say "poor thing" about the patient. This is her eleventh visit to
fix her deformed face and nothing has worked. The doctor says "each of us is
afforded as much opportunity as possible to fit into society." People have an
obligation to conform in this society.

One of the options for "people of your kind" is to be segregated from society, he tells Miss Tyler. She says it's "a ghetto designed for freaks." The doctor
says "the state is not unsympathetic."

But why does the state care? Miss Tyler says "who are you people anyway—
what is the state? Who makes all these rules[8] and statutes that people who are
different have to stay away . . . ?" She says the state "hasn't the right to make
ugliness a crime." The doctor wonders why people can't be different and the
nurse cautions saying that talk could be treason.

The Leader of the state comes on TV which is broadcast in the hospital. He
speaks of "Glorious Conformity" about "the delight and ultimate pleasure of
our unified society." Meanwhile, Miss Tyler's bandages come off. While cutting
them the doctor drops the scissors he is so startled. The attempt to correct
her face has failed and she is summoned to the colony. The doctor notes that
"under certain circumstances . . . the state does provide for the extermination
of undesirables."

When the bandages are taken off Miss Tyler is a classic beauty and it is the
doctor and nurses who are deformed pug nosed people. Miss Tyler starts to
run through the hospital corridor where we see The Leader still speaking on
conformity and unity: "we know now that there must be a single purpose,
a single norm, a single approach, a single entity of people, a single virtue, a
single morality, a single frame of reference, a single philosophy of government." He continues "it is essential to society that we not only have a norm
but that we conform to that norm . . . differences weaken us." Only conformity
is praised.

Miss Tyler runs into a room with Mr. Smith, a leader of a village group for
others. Mr. Smith is handsome. He convinces Miss Tyler to go with him to be
with "your own kind." What the pug-nosed people consider ugly we consider
beautiful and vice versa. Mr. Smith tells Miss Tyler that "beauty is in the eye
of the beholder."

"Number 12 Looks Just Like You" (written by Charles Beaumont and John
Tomerlin and based on the story "The Beautiful People" by Beaumont) continues this theme of conformity as dictated by the state where the state com-

pels everyone to get a makeover to be beautiful. For Tocqueville, the "tyranny of the majority" was a concept that applied to the influence that society has over individuals to conform. For Serling, in the worst society, this influence to conform would be dictated by the state. Perhaps Serling saw that the state would become so powerful that it would be able to dictate to the individual even how he or she looks, whereas Tocqueville saw the rise of the powerful bureaucratic state. For Tocqueville society would have more influence over such things as looks.

In "Number 12" a girl named Marilyn and her mother are looking at "patterns" of models that everyone can look like. Marilyn is perplexed, so her mother offers her a glass of "instant smile" Serling comes on and says "let's call it the year 2000" when science can make everyone look the way he or she wants. Serling seems to suggest that in 2000 people would be obsessed with their looks, clearly he saw into the future of plastic surgery, makeover reality shows and the importance of conformity to a standard of beauty.

Marilyn, the heroine of "Number 12," wants to be ugly because she associates ugliness with individuality and non conformity. Marilyn's society is a society in which everyone is beautiful which means no one is beautiful. For Plato, Beauty did not exist in the world of appearances but in the world of ideas that were essential and unchanging. While Plato decries superficiality Serling decried conformity probably for Tocquevillian reasons though it has been suggested that Serling's distaste for conformity may be either anti-communist or anti-McCarthy in origin.[9]

Marilyn admits to reading Socrates who also placed little importance on looks. Because she likes to read books and discuss ideas and because she shuns outward appearances she is considered "a very sick girl." If Marilyn gets the makeover—to look like Number 12—she won't have individuality—how is anyone going to know her?

Marilyn decides not to have the makeover and says "I won't let them change me" but her doctor, hired by the state, says "being like everyone else" is a sign of maturity and "plays an important role in psychological adjustment." Marilyn's mother, who has had the makeover, says that Marilyn's father was against the makeover and "had some rather nonconformist ideas."

Because Marilyn does not want the makeover she is sent, again probably by the state, to Prof. Sigmund Friend who wears a shirt that says "Sig" and has a German accent, to change her mind and "make the necessary corrections. He says it's "for your own good—why else would the state go to such trouble and expense?" His soliloquy continues: "Many years ago wiser men than I decided to try and eliminate the reasons for inequality and injustice in this world of ours. They saw in physical unattractiveness one of the factors which made men hate. So they charged the finest scientific minds with the task of eliminating ugliness. . . ." This sounds like Tocqueville's concept of the welfare state "taking all the trouble of thinking" from individuals. We find out later that if people look alike, they also think alike—which gives more power to the state because it takes an independent thinker to go against the state. Professor Friend reminds Marilyn that her discussion of the dignity of the individual is considered "subversive."

Marilyn's next remark is straight from Plato. She quotes her father "when everyone is beautiful no one will be because without ugliness there can be no beauty" and says "he cared about . . . his dignity as a human being . . . he . . . killed himself because . . . they took away his identity. . . ." For Plato, Beauty must have its opposite, Ugliness, in order to be Beauty. So if everyone is beautiful, no one is beautiful. If everyone is tall, everyone is also short.

Marilyn understands that when the state does a makeover it takes away one's ability to think. Again this is Tocqueville—the state takes away all incentive to think because it's in the state's interest that the individual not think. The totalitarian state prizes conformity in thought, word and looks.

Marilyn tries to escape but is taken to a room and has the makeover. She now looks just like her friend Val. Serling's voiceover says "these and other strange blessings may be waiting in the future." Tocqueville would agree that this is a "strange blessing" of the state—just like other goods and services the state provides so the individual not think. Serling's point is that changing the way people look doesn't eliminate prejudice—it just gives the state too much power. The same holds true in "The Trade-Ins" where the Holts, an elderly couple, go to the New Life Corp to trade in "old bodies for new." The New Life Corp "deals in youth" according to the salesman and promises "bodies that are prefect in composition, concept, construction."

The Holts, John and Marie, are shown models to select from. There is an entire showroom of youthful models. The "prototypes" are "invested" with "memory bank, personality, continuity." The Holts are not doing it for looks but for health reasons, but the message is clear. Serling says they are people "in their twilight years who are about to find that there happens to be a zone with the same name."

The Holts choose two models—they can have them for a week on approval and if they don't like it they can go back to the way they were. The trade is $10,000 for two people. But the Holts only have $5000 so they decide to get the trade in for Mr. Holt. Mr. Holt says "I'm not good at anything anymore . . . not worth anything to anybody." Mr. Holt gets the trade in for the body of a man many decades younger, but now he is too young for Marie. John changes back—they decide that they'd rather be together the way they were.

"The Trade-Ins" has themes of Plato, including the idea of the body as the prison of the soul and the unimportance of appearances, but also from De Tocqueville—in a society that prizes the young, people pay to change their appearance, be young and conform. By doing this we have eliminated individuality which, Serling considers, may be detrimental to society and to democracy. If conformity is valued individuals won't find it important to have individual ideas, thoughts and opinions and democracy may just be a collection of people who think the same ideas.

Alexis de Tocqueville spoke of the dangers of conformity, of the "Tyranny of the Majority" and Serling clearly agrees. His character "Mr. Bevis" is an example of eccentric non conformity that Serling praises. Mr. James B.W. Bevis is a cute eccentric, Serling calls him an "oddball" whose "tastes lean toward stuffed animals, zither music, professional football, Charles Dickens, mooseheads, carnivals, dogs . . ." and he is "discombooberated." But Serling says "without him, without his warmth, without his kindness the world would be a considerably poorer place."

Mr. Bevis, a non-conformist, has an apartment that is filled with junk like a birdcage. He wears a bow tie and slides down the banister, rolling out onto the street to the music of an organ grinder. His car is a wreck.

Bevis works in an office, a secretarial pool, a frequent symbol of conformity for Serling, where his eccentricity interferes with his work and he gets fired because of the way he dresses and decorates his desk with junk. His car gets hit and he is evicted because he can't pay his rent.

After Mr. Bevis gets fired he goes to a bar and meets a guardian angel, Mr. J. Hardy Hampstead. Hardy Hampstead says he can change the day so that Bevis won't be fired—he explains that this requires a personality and wardrobe change. Bevis will have to conform. He puts Bevis in a conservative suit. The "new" Bevis walks down the stairs, he doesn't slide down the banister. He pays his rent and drives a sports car.

In order to be successful he can't listen to zither music. He drives to work in his sports car and arrives to a clean and boring desk with no carnival clock, no model ship. The boss announces that Mr. Bevis has been given a raise. Bevis fits in but is now boring. He is successful but he is not happy. He has abandoned his individuality, exactly what De Tocqueville warned of in Democracy in America "What Sort of Despotism Democratic Nations have to fear": "For their happiness such a government willingly labors . . . what remains, but to spare them all the care of thinking? . . ."

Mr. Bevis decides that his individuality is worth more than the raise his boss gave him for conforming. Hampstead turns him back into himself. He gets fired again and is back at the bar but now he appreciates his individuality. It's not worth being a conformist. Bevis lives in his own Twilight Zone according to Serling, but makes things interesting.

Capital Punishment

While Serling is clearly anti-war ("A Quality of Mercy," "The Purple Testament," "Third from the Sun," "Probe 7," "No Time Like the Past") it is not clear that he is anti–capital punishment. In "Execution" the scene is a group of cowboys gathering around a tree 1880 for a "necktie party" where violent criminal Joe Caswell is about to be hanged. The victim's father says he wants justice and he wants Caswell to pay and maybe Serling agrees—this story shows that perhaps Serling does think of hanging in terms of justice.

When Caswell is hanged he vanishes and travels ahead through time where he sees a scientist (played by Russell Johnson who played The Professor on *Gilligan's Island*). He is the first time traveler.

Caswell is perplexed by his new surroundings.[10] The scientist explains that ideas about right and wrong don't change, justice doesn't change saying "some things don't change—ideas, concepts things like right and wrong . . . what about justice?" He realizes that Caswell was about to be hanged as a murderer and in order to have justice he must send Caswell back. Caswell explains that what is justice now isn't the same as justice in the 1800s when he had to kill people saying he killed "a whole territory" and "stopped counting after 20." After, he kills the scientist.

Caswell walks around New York City and goes into a bar where he breaks a juke box. He shows the bartender a gun and orders a beer. He sees a cowboy on TV and shoots the TV. The bartender calls the police and Caswell shoots at them.

Caswell finds his way back to the scientist's time machine where a thug pulls a gun on him to rob him. Caswell fights with him and the thug strangles Caswell with a rope from the curtains. The thug sees the time machine and steps in—he is transported back to the tree and the cowboys where he is seen hanging from the noose that was meant for Caswell. Justice transcends time. Apparently Serling believes that capital punishment is justified if someone (Caswell) murders 20 people—or if the execution is done by "fate" and not the state. Caswell's murderer is also executed.

But Serling suggests that capital punishment is not justified even for criminals such as Nazis if the state is doing it. Serling is against capital punishment if it's done by the state, but he's not against the universe carrying out "justice."[11] He's not against retribution for criminals, but apparently he is against state sponsored executions.

His belief regarding capital punishment is brought out in "Deaths-Head Revisited" where a former Nazi official returns to Dachau and is confronted by a former prisoner. The Nazi says he followed orders. He is tried for crimes against humanity, having killed 1700 human beings. He sees the ghosts of Dachau. He is convicted, but sentenced only to be "rendered insane." Serling's voiceover reminds us that the state can turn against the individual—and that it's not just possible in the Twilight Zone, but everywhere. So this is Serling's plea against the distortion of state power, but also it would seem against the power of the state to execute the guilty—even if they are Nazis and mass murderers.

The theme against capital punishment is continued in "Dust" which is set in a Mexican border town, probably Texas, in the old West. Serling opens the show standing in front of a hangman's rope. There is a Mexican man named Luis who is in jail waiting to be hanged. He is taunted by a charlatan medicine man named Mr. Sykes who says that Luis was drunk when his wagon ran over and killed a little girl.

Luis does not deny that he was drunk when he ran over the little girl. The jailer, presumably the voice of Serling, is sad that there is going to be a hanging. The condemned man's father and daughter confront the victim's parents and the girl, Estrellita, says that they are sorry for the accident. Luis' father offers him a lucky coin and says that because of poverty Luis drank too much and ran over the girl.

Sykes sees an opportunity to take advantage of Luis' superstitious father and situation by selling him "magic dust" that turns hate to love and costs 100 pesos. The sheriff, commenting on man's inhumanity to man, says "when was it God made people—on the 6th day? He should have stopped on the 5th."

They gather at the hanging booth, the noose around Luis' neck. Just then his father buys the magic dust from Sykes, and throws it on the crowd so the people will be compassionate. Sykes laughs knowing it's a trick. Luis is hanged—but the rope breaks. The victim's parents take it as a sign of divine intervention and the sheriff asks them if they want to call off the hanging. "What about it?" he says. They agree. Luis has suffered enough. They decide that "one victim is enough" and there is no execution. Compassion prevents them from hanging Luis—who was guilty not of intentional murder. We can infer that Serling is against capital punishment carried out by the state. For Serling, the individual is above the state, the individual created the state—not vice versa, so the state cannot execute the individual.

The themes of capital punishment and racism are also in "I Am the Night—Color Me Black" where a man is executed for killing a racist and blackness covers the countryside to protest the execution. It's execution day in a small Midwestern town. The town clock rings 7:30am but it's "pitch black outside." The deputy Pierce wonders "what's going on?" The Sheriff, Charlie Koch, doesn't know. The townspeople speculate "it's the end of the world."

Who is to be executed? A man named Jagger (sounds like dagger) and his crime is shooting a "cross burning psychopathic bully" in what seems like self defense. Jagger describes himself as the "village idiot who tries to be his brother's keeper" and the cross burner as a "psychopath who handled the whipping of some poor scared colored guy."

The townspeople gather with lanterns at 9am and say of the dark "it's just plain weird." The deputy and sheriff arrive and the deputy looks at the noose and remarks "that oughtta tend to him" and the sheriff asks "who or what is going to tend to us?" The Editor of the newspaper suggests they "dispense with business as usual" because "there's something odd going on around here." The sheriff suggests he gave into a mob of townspeople who wanted Jagger convicted of murder.

A black preacher comes to talk to the town editor at the scene of the execution. The editor says of Jagger "he is a very lonely man, but he won't be lonely anymore" suggesting that many of those executed have been wrongly executed and were good people.[12] The preacher tells Jagger "you and I are . . . obviously a different color but you stood up for me and mine you spoke for us and . . . you killed for us." The mob wants Jagger executed, he won't apologize for killing the cross burner. The preacher is sorry that Jagger has no remorse. Jagger accuses the preacher of playing to the mob, the "majority" and the preacher says "that's all there is is the majority—the minority must have died on the cross 2000 years ago."

The preacher addresses the mob "you hated and you killed" the black is "the hate" everyone feels so much that they had to "vomit it out." It gets even darker.

Back at the police station the news over the radio is that it is dark over the Berlin Wall, China, North Vietnam, Birmingham, Alabama, a political prison in Budapest. Serling's voiceover: "a sickness known as hate . . . highly contagious . . . don't look for it in the Twilight Zone, look for it in the mirror . . . before the light goes out altogether."[13]

In "I Am the Night" Serling sees killing as killing—whether it's the individual or the state, whether it's killing a racist or the racist's killer, and both are wrong. The preacher's speech to the crowd includes this idea—that capital punishment is more hate, (even for the killing of a cross burner) and the blackness is in protest of the state's offense.[14]

In the French film, "An Occurrence at Owl Creek Bridge," written by Robert Enrico based on a short story by Ambrose Bierce, a confederate soldier is going to be hanged by Union soldiers.

The noose is strung from a bridge. They put the noose around his neck. He is standing on a plank and when they take away the plank he'll fall into the water. A twig floats by—it's freer than him.

He thinks of his wife on a southern plantation. He starts to cry. They step off the plank and the rope breaks—he hits the water and freedom. He sees the trees, he sees a spider and a worm in the water. Things he would not think are beautiful are beautiful to him. The soldiers try to shoot him and say "he mustn't escape" but he swims to freedom. He runs into the forest and home to the plantation. He runs towards his wife and she is wearing a hoop skirt. Just as he is about to touch her the scene flashes back to the bridge and he is hanged. Though Serling didn't write this it seems to be anti capital punishment—just when the prisoner is having a daydream and is almost home, like Joey Crown or Bolie Jackson in "The Big Tall Wish," there is no magic here. Clearly, Serling would have preferred the rope break, like in "Dust," particularly because we don't know if this man is guilty.

Justice and the Law

If the state cannot execute the individual, the individual cannot distribute justice without laws or the backing of the state. This is apparent in "Four O'clock" where in the opening scene we see a man in a darkened room with an eyeshade and a parrot. He is talking on the telephone. But he is up to no good. He is calling employees to tell them that their employees are "Communists" and "subversives." He calls businesses and schools telling them that their employees are "morally questionable."

This man, Oliver Crangle, decides that at four o'clock there will be the end of "immorality" Serling calls him an "avenging angel." He takes it upon himself to mete out justice. He is the judge and jury. He renders the sentence. He tells his landlady to respect his privacy, but he doesn't respect anyone else's. Crangle decides who is "impure" and must be punished. At four o'clock Crangle will "expose evil."

A doctor's wife comes to see Crangle. Her husband, Curt J. Lucas, is being harassed by Crangle because "he has done a lot against society." Mrs. Lucas asks Crangle "by what right do you presume" to make these judgments? Crangle explains it's not personal and that he won't put up with evil including "communists, subversives, thieves." At four o'clock he'll make all the "evil people" two feet tall. Crangle looks at the clock—it's 3:30pm. He has a copy of the Gettysburg address on the wall and crosses out the phrase "all men are created equal."[15] Finally, a man named Mr. Hall from the FBI comes to see Crangle. He is an agent of the state. Crangle has called them and has even called "Washington" but says "that call probably won't even go through" because "the reds are in complete control in Washington." Mr. Hall wants to know if Mr. Crangle has ever had any "psychiatric help" and says the FBI can't help him. Crangle tells Hall that when he shrinks the "evil people" you'll "have to build more jails, more electric chairs, gallows."

Mr. Hall tells Crangle that in the United States "the law" makes all of this unnecessary. Crangle tells Hall that he is a subversive and is going to be two feet tall. The clock strikes four, Pete the parrot squawks, and Crangle himself becomes two feet tall.

The moral is clear—when the individual tries to put himself above the law and above the purpose of the state (which is to administer the law impartially) he gets punished. Hall echoes Aristotle when he says "The law, Mr. Crangle. We have the law. We like people's help, their support their cooperation, but interference is quite another matter." As Aristotle said in *The Politics*, Book III chapter XV "law contains no element of passion" and the purpose of the state is to make and administer impartial law.

Tom Paine said "in America, the law is king."[16] Locke said that the purpose of the state is to make and administer law impartially. In "You Drive" (written by Earl Hamner, Jr.) Mr. Alexander Pope puts himself above the law and tries to get away with homicide.

Oliver Pope is driving home one day when he hits and kills a boy on a bicycle. He stops, looks around, gets back in his car and drives off. But a woman in a phone booth sees him. He goes home and tries to pretend it didn't happen. He talks about competition at work while his wife sees the car's lights flashing on and off in the garage. When she asks him if he's seen the newspaper he realizes it was the newspaper boy he hit.

In the middle of the night the car horn starts honking and wakes Mr. Pope up. He goes to the garage and disconnects the horn. His wife is the voice of justice saying that she hopes the perpetrator gets "what's coming to him."

Mr. Pope stays home, the car keeps honking in the garage. His wife takes the car out and it stops at the place where Mr. Pope hit the boy, at 3rd and Park. She uses the pay phone to call a tow truck. The car goes to the shop but is back in the garage honking. It's driven itself back to the house.

Mr. Pope starts to get paranoid. His co worker comes to see him with work but Ollie tells him to stop "bucking for my job." The colleague knows the boy who was hit. He drives to the scene of the accident while driving home and is stopped by a policeman. A witness says he hit the boy. They arrest Pete Radcliffe, the wrong man, and Mr. Pope is off the hook for the hit and run but his car keeps honking in the garage.

The car wakes Mr. Pope up and he goes to the garage. The bumper clangs to the ground and the car starts by itself. The car radio goes on and announces the arrest of Peter Radcliffe—over and over. The lights go on and off—Mr. Pope smashes them. The horn honks. He tries to destroy the car but the car wants justice.

Mr. Pope decides to take the bus to work saying "I don't trust that car." He wants to sell the car so "somebody'll take it off our hands" just like somebody took the accident off his hands.

As he starts walking to the bus the garage door opens and the car drives out and follows him. When it reaches him it stops and waits for him to get in.

He tries to run away but it starts to storm and he slips and is almost run over by the car. As he is lying in the street the passenger door opens and he gets in. The car drives to the police station and lets him out. Serling's voiceover says "all persons attempting to conceal criminal acts involving their cars are hereby warned: check first to see that underneath that chrome there does not lie a conscience."

In "You Drive" a parallel is drawn between Mr. Pope's criminal activity and capitalist competition. After the accident Mr. Pope (ironically named) complains to his wife about competition at the office. He is paranoid about Peter Radcliffe trying to take his job while he is paranoid about being caught for the accident. But Peter Radcliffe is the good guy (when he comes to see Mr. Pope at home he has written all of Mr. Pope's letters and has spent the day doing Mr. Pope's work!) and nice guys finish last in the competitive capitalist state—even to the point of taking the rap for Mr. Pope.

The message is that the unscrupulous and competitive capitalist tries to circumvent the law. In such a world, where everything is based on competition and chance as Woody Allen says some other entity must take responsibility for enforcing the law—in this case it's Mr. Pope's car. This story echoes the them of "A Thing about Machines" in which Bartlett Finchley's car runs him down thereby proving him right about the power of machines. In "You Drive," Mr. Pope's car has the power to do good by making him follow the law and by bringing justice to the story. This is very important, because in the absence of justice we cannot have a Lockean society or an Aristotelian one where the state makes and enforces laws and in the absence of law we cannot have justice. But, for Serling, in the absence of good behavior something must make it right.

"What You Need" reinforces Serling's emphasis on justice and punishment particularly when it is not being dished out by the state. The intro says that Fred Renard is a "sour man" who is siting at a café when a salesman walks in. The salesman sizes up customers and gives them "what they need." (even though he is a salesman with a suitcase of stuff he never seems to take money). He gives one lady cleaning fluid because as he says "it's what you need." She uses it to clean the jacket of a baseball player named Lefty.

Meanwhile, Renard watches and follows the salesman into the street. He pursues him in a menacing way and threatens him and asks "what do I need?" The salesman gives him scissors which he uses to cut his scarf when it gets caught in the elevator.

When the salesman returns home he sees Renard is in his room and is waiting for him. He harasses and intimidates the salesman and asks him how he can see what people need. The salesman gives Renard a leaky pen that leaks next to the name of a horse that is going to race. Renard bets on the horse and wins $240. Renard tries it again but the pen doesn't work.

Renard goes back to the salesman and threatens him. The salesman, Pedott, says he can't sell him anything more. Renard steals a pair of shoes from Pedott and puts them on. He threatens Pedott again and as he runs away after Pedott he slips and a car runs over him. Pedott says that Renard was going to kill him so what Pedott needed for Mr. Renard was "slippery shoes" in a hit and run.

"What You Need" shows Serling's preoccupation with justice and punishment and even capital punishment when it is justice from "the Twilight Zone" as opposed to capital punishment by the state. In fact, several of the shows include this idea that punishment is good when someone has been wronged—as in "You Drive" and "Four O'clock"—but not capital punishment in "Dust" and "I Am the Night" where the blackness indicates nature's against it.

The preoccupation with justice and punishment is seen also in "The Encounter," written by Martin M. Goldsmith and not syndicated. This is one of the most bizarre and confusing shows, yet it clearly demonstrates again this theme—as Serling said in "The Execution" "justice can span years. Retribution is not subject to a calendar."

This story is about vengeance after war. Mr. Fenton, a WWII veteran, is working in his attic and he sees a Samurai sword. As he throws it across the room a Japanese man, Arthur Takamuri, knocks on the door and asks if Fenton needs a gardener. Fenton invites him in for a beer. They argue back and forth, with Takamuri saying that he's "just as much American as anybody."

Fenton sees his WWII uniform and mentions that he fought in Okinawa where he took the Samurai sword from a Japanese officer. There is an inscription in Japanese on the sword that Arthur says he cannot read but when Fenton goes to get the beer Arthur picks up the sword and says "I'm going to kill him."

Serling calls Fenton "a veteran of yesterday's war" noting that WWII was "20 years ago." Even though Fenton taunts Arthur he says "the war's over" but he sees that the sword is missing. Fenton suggests that Arthur could use the sword to kill him—he knows the inscription says "the sword will avenge me." He asks Arthur to tell him where he hid the sword. Fenton hears voices from the war and Arthur almost stabs him but gives him the sword.

Arthur accuses Fenton of shooting the Japanese soldier after he surrendered and Fenton admits that he did. Arthur tries to leave but the door is barricaded.[17] Fenton says "it looks like you're not supposed to leave just yet."

They go back to the attic and Arthur picks up the sword, revealing that he was at Pearl Harbor when it was bombed but his father was a traitor. Fenton rails about being laid off as a construction worker because they could get cheap labor—"they're lettin' 'em in from everywhere . . . Japan . . . foreigners" He goes on to disparage Asians saying "women are a dime a dozen—anybody that's been in the Orient knows that."

Arthur is now eyeing the sword again, he says to Fenton "you're a murderer. You killed a defenseless man." Fenton says "In the Pacific we were told that you guys weren't even human you were some species of an ape."

The denouement is confusing. It's not clear if Arthur stabs Fenton but Fenton is stabbed by the sword which Arthur then pulls from him. With sword in hand Arthur yells "banzai" and leaps out the window kamikaze style and probably leaps to his death. Fenton has said earlier that they are two floors up and it's too high to jump out the window. Serling's voiceover: "Two men in an attic . . . their common bond and their common enemy guilt. . . ."

Both Fenton and Arthur are guilty—Fenton's guilt from his shooting the Japanese soldier who had surrendered and Arthur's from his family treachery. Because they are both guilty and because it seems as if Arthur's father did not pay for his treachery, both must be sacrificed—Fenton for "war crimes" and Arthur for his father's "war crimes." As Serling has said retribution and justice are "not subject to a calendar." Both Fenton and Arthur get capital punishment, but not from the state. For Serling, capital punishment is ok if the state is not doing it, that is if it's done by the Twilight Zone.

The social contract theorists, Hobbes, Locke and Rousseau, support capital punishment for murder, Hobbes saying that you may kill in self-defense and Locke quoting the Bible. For Rousseau the social contract is based on this— "so that we are not murdered, we agree to capital punishment if we murder." He says in the "Social Contract," Book II, ch. 5 "it is in order that we may not fall victims to an assassin that we consent to die if we ourselves turn assassins. In this treaty, so far from disposing of our own lives, we think only of securing them. . . ."

As Serling said in "Execution" "justice can span years. Retribution is not subject to a calendar" and this is the theme of "Deaths-Head Revisited" where a Nazi is punished for his crimes against humanity.

Here, Mr. Schmidt, who is really SS Captain Lutze, checks into a hotel in Dachau, 8 miles NW of Munich for nostalgia—he was a captain in the SS 17 years ago. He goes to Dachau, like a school reunion for him, and he fondly remembers his glory days as a Nazi. He says he had "good times" there. He goes into some of the empty buildings—he remembers not giving water to a prisoner. As he is walking he sees a former prisoner, he remembers him as Alfred Becker, and says he looks the same. Becker is wearing his striped Dachau prisoner uniform.

Lutze hears ghostly sounds from the abandoned building and wants to leave—he tells Becker that he came back for "nostalgia" and can't they forget the past, but Becker tells him no. Becker says he has business to do—the court is convening for Lutze's trial. Lutze calls it "nonsense." He is being tried for "crimes against humanity." He used to torture Becker, now the ghosts of the

Dachau prisoners confront him. He bangs the door to get out and the inmates of compound 6 indict him on counts including murder.

Lutze faints—was it a hallucination? Now he sees Becker. The trial wasn't a dream. Lutze is guilty but he laughs and wonders how ghosts see "that justice is done." He remembers that he killed Becker the night Dachau was liberated. The jury sentences him to be rendered insane. Becker says that it's "not hatred", but "retribution." "Not revenge," but "justice." Indeed, as Serling said in "Execution" "justice can span years. Retribution is not subject to a calendar" and neither is justice for crimes against humanity.

War

Just as he shows an aversion for capital punishment Serling shows anti-war sentiment in *The Twilight Zone* in shows like "The Passersby," "The Encounter," "A Quality of Mercy," and "No Time Like the Past." The experience of going to war after high school was, according to a former secretary "the thing he felt most deeply about."[18]

In "The Passersby" soldiers are walking on a road that is "the aftermath of the Civil War." There are wounded soldiers coming home from war. They walk by the house of a southern woman sitting on her porch. She gives them water. They talk about the glory of the old south. One soldier says "war claims a lot of victims." War is "trumpets and drums, nothing but trumpets and drums" when soldiers go to war.

The passersby comprise a parade day and night of soldiers coming home from war. One of the soldiers befriends the woman sitting on the porch and says his father was proud because he was "marching off to war to become a man" but says "he came back half a man."

The woman on the porch laments that the Yankees took away her way of life and wonders what happened to the soldier who killed her husband. She tells the soldier she befriended that she has a gun and that she wants to kill a Yankee "a bullet in exchange for the one my husband took." She takes out her rifle and threatens to kill a Yankee soldier. She shoots at him, but nothing happens. He is a ghost. All the passersby are ghosts including her and Lincoln, who leads her on the road of the passersby.

In "The Passersby" there is no mention made of the purpose or necessity of war—only the results—the march of ghosts from the Civil War which, we may infer, may not be worth the effort. Nor is it mentioned that sometimes not going to war is worse than going to war.

For Hobbes, there is no morality in war. War is a condition whereby everyone fights with everyone—the "war of all against all" as in "A Quality of Mercy" "in war you kill."

Serling likes to think otherwise. In "Still Valley" the scene is Virginia in 1863 during the Civil War. Two confederate soldiers are sitting around a campfire waiting to be besieged by Yankees. One of the soldiers, Joseph Paradine, goes down to the valley to scout.

In the valley he sees soldiers who are frozen like mannequins. There is an entire regiment. Paradine finds this most awesome. He meets an old man who explains it. The man has a book that he says he used on the Yankee regiment—it is a book of witchcraft. The man invokes the devil and freezes Paradine. What he did to the Yankees he can do to the whole Union army with magic.

The old man gives the book of witchcraft to Paradine so that he may freeze the Yankees and win the Civil War. Paradine goes back to his camp with the book where he is able to do the incantation and freeze Yankees. One soldier asks Paradine to do the incantation and put a spell on all the Yankees—it's the only way for the south to win the Civil War. Paradine decides he can't win by using the devil, and burns the book. The next day the Union wins the Civil War.

Serling likes the idea of fair play, even in war—if something is against morality or "human rights" then it should not be done even in war. This is not the Hobbesian view of war—for Serling we should try to be decent even in indecent circumstances like war. Perhaps this is a fantasy of Serling, though criminal prosecutions for "war crimes" would probably be along the lines of this thinking.

This idea of compassion in wartime and anti-war sentiment is also apparent in "A Quality of Mercy" and "The Purple Testament" where soldiers put themselves in other soldiers' shoes.

"The Purple Testament" is set in the Philippine Islands in 1945 during WWII. There is a great intro by Serling "these are the faces of the young men who fight as if some omniscient painter had mixed a tube of oils that were at one time earth brown, dust grey, blood red, beard black and fear yellow white . . . for this is the province of combat and these are the faces of war."

Two soldiers are talking—Lieutenant William "Fitz" Fitzgerald is speaking with the Captain who is asking him why he looks so bad. Four soldiers were killed "these four men were all under 21." Something has gotten to Fitz. He hands Captain Phil a list of 4 men whose names he wrote before they went into battle. He looked into their faces and saw "a light." This torments Fitz. He can stand in front of a platoon "and know which ones aren't coming back."

Lieutenant Fitz visits his friend Smitty in the hospital and when he looks at his face he sees the light. Now he looks at the Captain and sees the light and tells him not to go. One of the commanders sums up the message "war stinks."

They are going to send Fitz for some rest when he looks in the mirror and sees the light on his face. The mirror falls and breaks. On the jeep ride out of the camp he is hit with a mine and blown up. Serling's voiceover from Shakespeare Richard III—"he has come to open the purple testament of bleeding war." Nobody wins.

"The Thirty Fathom Grave" demonstrates the psychological effects of war. The scene is the south pacific in 1963 and officers have to go 30 fathoms to see what is making a noise in a sunken submarine. The chief boatswain's mate, Bell, is acting strangely. He feels that he is being pulled someplace and the captain wants a diver to go down and get the number from the submarine hull.

The diver goes down twice, and sees a number (714) on the side of the submarine. The captain looks in a book with hull numbers and sees that the sub was commissioned Dec 1941 and sunk in action August 7, 1942. They wonder who is inside the submarine.

Meanwhile, the medic talks to the captain about Bell—he has delusions and needs psychiatric help. The captain says "all of a sudden he cracks up like a dinghy in a storm." Bell is in sick bay when he looks in the mirror and sees the souls of the sunken shipmates staring back beckoning him. The noise continues.

The captain calls for a sub rescue ship. Bell opens the door and sees the souls of the shipmates beckoning him. The medic walks into the hall and there's seaweed. They send the diver down again and he gets no response, but Bell's dogtags which he lost 20 years ago in WWII. That was Bell's submarine. He was supposed to put in an infrared signal light to hide the submarine, but he didn't and the Japanese hit them. Bell's negligence made the Japanese hit the submarine. Bell is the only survivor of the crew. He was responsible but he got out. He feels guilty—the sunken souls are beckoning him because he says he should be there with them. Bell jumps overboard to be with his crewmates on the submarine. The captain says "sometimes I think that's the worst thing there is about war . . . not just what it does to the bodies, what it does to the minds" and Serling says "look for this one filed under H for haunting in the Twilight Zone." Though Serling's anti-war sentiment is included in these episodes he, like Hobbes, sees war as part of human nature. As Captain Benteen says in "On Thursday" to a group assembled on another planet "we thought we could escape war."

"No Time Like the Past" also has an anti-war theme that comes out as Paul Driscoll eats dinner with other residents of his nineteenth-century boarding house. Paul asks to be transported back to the nineteenth century because it is a time before bombs and World Wars. But one of the residents is very pro-war and wants American imperialism. Paul and his friend Abby, a schoolteacher, disagree, and he mocks them as "pacifists" a term which he holds in contempt.

Paul Driscoll then says if the boarding resident is offended by pacifists, he is offended by "armchair warriors" who send young men to war. Driscoll rejects the idea that a country becomes strong by sending young men to war and

Abby agrees saying "patriotism doesn't have to come with pain." They leave the table and the two boarding house residents at the table refer to Paul as a "violent man."

Two other shows, "In Praise of Pip" and "The 7th is Made Up of Phantoms," one about war and one about magic, include both a pro and anti war message.

In "The 7th is Made Up of Phantoms" the National Guard is on maneuvers and the soldiers step back in time to Custer and Little Big Horn in 1876. They see a "wigwam" where the 7th cavalry fought the Sioux Indians. The wind blows and they are blown back to 1876. Now they see smoke signals and hear drums. A horse comes galloping over the hill.

But there's no anti-war message here. Their leader doesn't know whether to "stop the Sioux massacre or join it." He calls the Lieutenant to get them. One of the soldiers thinks the other two are hallucinating and leaves, but sees more wigwams—the fog of war, a mirage. But one of the soldiers is hit by an arrow. They go over the hill to Little Big Horn and vanish.

The other soldiers from the National Guard go looking for them but the Lieutenant sees their names on the Custer Battlefield Monument. The captain says that they should have had a tank to use against the Sioux. And the Lieutenant says "what?" and the captain says "never mind" and claims he didn't say anything even though he wanted Custer to use the tank against the Indians. Perhaps Serling here says that if you want to win a war you must use tanks—learning from his WWII experience.

Also from the fifth season, "In Praise of Pip," though not a war show, includes an anti-war message: we shouldn't be in Vietnam.

Does Size Matter?

The ant finds kingdoms in a foot of ground.

—Steven Vincent Benet

"It's a Good Life" is a story about the individual and the state, a little boy plays the part of the state that forces individuals to conform and keep their thoughts to the party line. The story (based on a story by Jerome Bixby) is set in Peeksville, Ohio, a town that is ruled by a "monster" who "moved an entire community back into the Dark Ages" by outlawing "automobiles, the electricity, the machines" and, most of all, singing. The monster is 6 year old Anthony Fremont.

Everybody has to smile and "think happy thoughts" or Anthony can make them disappear. Serling's voiceover says that Anthony is "absolutely in charge." Everyone panders to Anthony for fear of being "wished into the cornfield" or banished. All the town's residents must be loyal to Anthony out of fear. The more dictatorial Anthony is the more the townspeople pledge their loyalty to him.

Anthony can read minds and can hear what people are thinking so people must not even think any negative thoughts or Anthony can punish them. To everything Anthony says people say "that's good, that's real good."

In the fashion of a dictator Anthony says "I hate anybody that doesn't like me" and anything that contradicts his thinking is outlawed or put into the cornfield. He dictates everything—what people watch on TV, what they eat, the weather.

At a birthday party for a friend, Dan, one of the gifts is a Perry Como record, but Anthony says Dan can't play it. Dan says "it's good I can't play it here." Another neighbor plays the piano while Dan becomes frustrated and drinks too much. Dan calls on the guests to overthrow Anthony and asks "some man in this room . . . willing to take a chance . . ." to "sneak up behind you and lay something heavy across your skull and end this once and for all." Nobody does. Dan says to the Fremonts "you and her, you had him. . . ."

Dan starts singing, which is not allowed, and calls Anthony a murderer. Anthony puts Dan's head on a jack-in-the-box and makes it snow on the crops—"but it's good that you're making it snow." Anthony says Dan "was a bad man" and wishes him into the cornfield.

Anthony behaves in "It's a Good Life" as a dictatorial state that defines dissent as "bad" and compliance as "good" and controls the individual with fear. This is how the dictatorial state gains "consent"—through coercion, the use of fear, and the use of force. It's not real consent, just forced manipulation of the individual through thought control, intimidation and fear.

"The Invaders" (written by Richard Matheson) is also about control, perhaps the control of the state over the individual using the imagery of size. This is perhaps the only *Twilight Zone* in which there is practically no dialogue, as in "Two" by Montgomery Pittman.

A woman who lives alone is cooking and hears a strange noise in the kitchen of her farmhouse. She goes outside and sees a spaceship or flying saucer. A little gangplank comes down from the saucer and little spacemen that look like toys walk out of the spacecraft. The woman is much bigger than them—but she is afraid of them. The spacemen have a gun that makes welts on her body. She throws something at them and retreats to her house.

She gets a wooden paddle for protection. Even though they are little she is afraid of them. She imagines that they are all over the house, she cowers in the corner and barricades the door. The little spaceman cuts her. She throws a spaceman in the fire and gets an ax. As she breaks up their ship a spaceman in the ship is overheard saying to the radio "race of giants here . . . too powerful." The camera focuses on the spaceship and it says "US Air Force." Serling says invaders are "from the tiny place called Earth . . . who would take the giant step across the sky" which is like "one small step for a man, one giant leap for mankind." The moral? Whoever is bigger has power—the state over the individual—except for Anthony Fremont and Napolean.[19]

"The Little People" continues the theme of "*L'Etat, c'est moi*" when two astronauts, Peter Craig and William Fletcher, land on a planet and Craig admits that he'd "like to give the orders." Craig encounters an entire civilization of miniature people on the planet. He towers and lords it over them because he is bigger than them. He puts them in fear by stepping on them to reinforce his rule.

When Fletcher fixes the spaceship so they can go to Earth Craig doesn't want to get on. He wants to stay where he is king. The little people have erected a statue to him in return for him not stepping on them. Fletcher leaves the planet alone so that Craig can rule the little people until another spaceship comes with astronauts that are giants and now he is the little person. They crush him and the little people pull down the statue they erected to him. Size is relative as is power.

What does Serling mean by his use of size as a symbol of power? Is it as Tom Paine said in *Common Sense* that the origin of monarchy is that the "principle ruffian" could conquer a territory because of his size which "obtained him the title of chief among plunderers" and that is why monarchy is not a legitimate form of government? Or is Serling saying something else?

Let's not forget that "The Little People" was written for season 3, 1961–1962, during the height of the American nuclear weapons buildup and the Cold War with the Soviet Union and Cuba. John F. Kennedy, a Democrat, was a staunch anti-communist and this was the key of his foreign policy. Perhaps he meant the "big" people are states with nuclear weapons and the "little" people are those states without them. Because Serling uses the theme of nuclear weapons in many of the shows this could be part of the theme of size—the size of a state's nuclear weapons and its power over other states without them.

The theme of power and size is continued in "Stopover in a Quiet Town" (written by Earl Hamner, Jr.). A man and a woman wake up and see they've gone to bed in their clothes. They went to a party the night before and are wearing party clothes. They're supposed to be on W. 12th St. in New York City—they left a party and drove home. But they wake up in a different room.

The couple had been drinking at the party so the wife drove home and remembers that "something came down on the car from overhead." Maybe it was an hallucination. They go into the kitchen and try to make a phone call but the phone is not wired. The drawers won't open, they are fake. The whole kitchen is fake. There's fake food in the refrigerator and they hear a child laughing.

They walk outside the house and still hear the child laughing. The husband remarks "I don't see how they stand it in this . . . burg." They see a squirrel—it's fake. They go to a neighbor's house, nobody's there. At a church they ring the bell but there's nobody there to hear it. They feel they're being watched. The wife says everything is fake. Even the grass is fake. A man in a car is a dummy.

They hear a train whistle and run to the station. They get on the train and it pulls out of the station, but goes around in a circle. They get out of the train and start to run—a giant hand reaches out and picks them up. It's a giant girl. She holds them in her hand and her mother says "be careful with your pets, dear, daddy brought them all the way from Earth." The girl puts them back in the pretend village.

"Stopover" continues the theme of interplanetary giants, the same theme from "The Invaders" (and also "The Fear") where the people from Earth are small and aliens are giants. Perhaps Serling's point is that a planet, or a state, with superior height—or weapons especially nuclear—is a superpower, has more power than the non nuclear states. So it pays to be a "giant" or have weapons of a giant, but Serling seems to think this gives one state or society an unfair advantage—as the giants in "Stopover "and "Little People" toy with Earthlings.

Hobbes called the state the "sovereign" and said that when people get together and give their power to an entity that is the social contract. On the cover of "Leviathan" the many individuals are combined in the Sovereign—"e pluribus unum" from many one—and there is a picture of the Sovereign with his sword and the many individuals who gave the sovereign power. Thus, the Sovereign is bigger than any individual but Hobbes says in ch. 18 of "Leviathan" Of Commonwealth that they are the "author of every act" of the Sovereign so he only acts to protect them: "but by this institution of a Commonwealth every particular man is author of all the Soveraigne doth."

For Hobbes, the state is a large individual by contract. The small individuals that make up the state retain some rights—including the right against self incrimination—but do not retain all the rights they had in the state of nature.

In the state of nature every individual was free and equal, and freedom was unlimited. This arrangement, while appealing, was not suitable because everyone being completely free also had the obligation to enforce justice. Again, while this might appeal to people nobody could get any business done because they were busy acting as police all the time and enforcing justice.

Therefore, according to Hobbes, the individuals agreed, in the state of nature, to transfer some of their rights onto a "Leviathan" or large person who would protect them so they could be free to do what they wanted. The Leviathan is the state that Hobbes said is merely a collection of individuals who, by contract, create a state which is a large person or artificial man.

Hobbes' theory is that every act of the sovereign is authored by the individuals who create the social contract so therefore the sovereign won't act against the individuals as the individuals would not act against themselves "but by this institution of a Commonwealth every particular man is author of all the Soveraigne doth."

But Serling's depiction is of the giant state not protecting but against the little individuals. It seems clear that Serling's point is Tocqueville's—beware of big government because if we've given government enough power to do good we've given it enough power to do bad.

In some sense Serling agrees with Aristotle—that "power goes with goodness" and you can be powerful even if you're not big if right and morality and goodness is on your side. Perhaps this is meant to illustrate that a big country is not necessarily strong because of that—it's goodness that's important. So a country can be small and good, or big and not powerful—the Soviet Union may be bigger than the United States but the United States is good.

Also, a country may be small but powerful because it has a nuclear bomb. This is illustrated in "The Last Night of a Jockey" a one person play starring Mickey Rooney as Grady, a jockey who's been suspended from riding because of "horse doping." We see him talking to himself (his "alter ego" or conscience) in the mirror of his room where the play is set. He thinks about his future. As his alter ego says "on a horse you're a man, on the ground you're a half pint."

The alter ego asks Grady what he wants and Grady says he wants to be big but Grady has no sense of what this means. Big can be unwieldy. Grady wakes up and he's big. He was five feet tall but now he can touch the ceiling. Grady is delighted. The alter ego asks "does size mean that much?" and Grady replies "you bet your bottom dollar."

Just then Mr. Newman, the lawyer from the racing commission, calls and says he's been reinstated as a jockey. The message is clear: it's not just Grady that's small—his dreams are. Size itself is meaningless—greatness is important, a theme also in "Four o'clock." Aristotle says "power goes with goodness" and Serling's voiceover says: "unfortunately for Mr. Grady he learned too late that you don't measure size with a ruler, you don't figure height with a yardstick . . . the giant is as he does. . . ." Serling said "if I have a preoccupation it is with conflict rather than with morality—the conflict of age versus youth, the lonely versus the mob." [20] And also the state versus the individual.

Notes

1. Quoted in CBS VHS video, *Treasures of the The Twilight Zone*, Oct. 1959.
2. Alexis de Tocqueville, *Democracy in America* (Random House, NY: 1981). Introduction by Thomas Bender "Why Democratic Nations show a more enduring love of Equality than of Liberty" p. 392–394, Vol II, Book II, ch. 1.
3. Alexis de Tocqueville, *Democracy in America*, Vol I, ch. xiv, "Unlimited Power of the Majority" p. 152.
4. Locke, *Second Treatise*, ch. 6, section 57.
5. Locke, *Second Treatise*, ch. 6, section 57.
6. Hobbes, *Leviathan*, ch. 30 Of Commonwealth.
7. Hobbes, *Leviathan*, "every subject is . . . Author of all the Actions, and Judgments of the Soveraigne" Of Commonwealth, ch. 18.
8. Miss Tyler uses the same phrase "you people" as Mr. Wordsworth in "The Obsolete Man" for the state.
9. Serling hated conformity perhaps because he feared it would lead to communism, a popular view in the 1950s and 60s when *The Twilight Zone* was written, or perhaps (according to Kristen Sanchez Carter) because he thought anti communists and the people who gave information to Sen. McCarthy were conformists. Carter suggested this idea at the SISSI conference in Colorado Springs, March 2008 and according to one commentator Serling was fresh from the McCarthy era and had friends affected by it, from "Submitted for Your Approval," *American Masters*, PBS TV show written by Thomas Wagner and John Goff and produced and directed by Susan Lacy, 1995.
10. Rousseau, *Discourse on the Origin of Inequality*. Rousseau says that if inventions are introduced people are perplexed "it appears that providence most wisely determined that the faculties, which he potentially possessed, should develop themselves only as occasion offered to exercise them in order that they might not be superfluous or perplexing to him, by appearing before their time, nor slow and useless when the need for them arose."
11. Another example, besides "Execution" is in "You Drive" when a man who has run over and killed a boy is brought to justice by car—the car drives him to the police station.
12. Is he referring to the Rosenbergs or the racial inequality of capital punishment?
13. This is one of the few that, like "Deaths-Head Revisited," doesn't end with the words "The Twilight Zone."
14. In an interview with the *LA Times* Serling said "In almost everything I've written, there is a thread of this: man's . . . need to dislike someone other than himself." Serling in "Creative Mainstream" by Ellen Cameron May, *LA Times*, June 25, 1967.
15. From Hobbes "NATURE hath made men so equal in the faculties of body and mind as that, though there be found one man sometimes manifestly stronger in body or of quicker mind than another, yet when all is reckoned together the difference between man and man is not so considerable as that one man can thereupon claim to himself any benefit to which another may not pretend as well as he" *Leviathan*, ch. 13.

16. Tom Paine, *Common Sense*, edited by Isaac Kramnick, p. 98.

17. This theme is seen in "The Obsolete Man" where two characters cannot leave the room.

18. Virginia Cox, quoted in Sander, p. 133.

19. This show can also be seen as "feminist" because it depicts a large woman who foils two small men. Serling also gives Julie Newmar a strong role, as the devil, in "Of Late I Think of Cliffordville."

20. *TV Guide* interview, April 21, 1962.

3

Fascism and Modernity

Automata—I Sing the Body Electric

FOR HOBBES, HUMANS ARE LIKE mechanical men or "automata" and in his Introduction to *Leviathan* he states:

> NATURE (the art whereby God hath made and governs the world) is by the art of man, as in many other things, so in this also imitated, that it can make an artificial animal. For seeing life is but a motion of limbs, the beginning whereof is in some principal part within, why may we not say that all automata(engines that move themselves by springs and wheels as doth a watch) have an artificial life? For what is the heart, but a spring; and the nerves, but so many strings; and the joints, but so many wheels, giving motion to the whole body, such as was intended by the Artificer? Art goes yet further, imitating that rational and most excellent work of Nature, man. For by art is created that great LEVIATHAN called a COMMONWEALTH, or STATE (in Latin, CIVITAS), which is but an artificial man, though of greater stature and strength than the natural, for whose protection and defence it was intended.[1]

This means that motion gives rise to and is the basis of the individual. All sense and thought, all emotions are based on motion.

Why is this important? It shows that Hobbes was influenced by "new science" and the science of Newton's physics in particular. He had a mechanistic view of the world—that not only could humans rely on science but they were science, and this modern view of the world is a rejection of soulcraft in favor of political science or statecraft. This sets the ground for the state as a contract and for a view of the world as scientific, rational and modern and for a view of the state as scientific and mechanistic. This is what makes Hobbes modern.

While the ancients had practiced "soulcraft" for Hobbes the state was man-made "statecraft" and science was the answer to how to make the world better. Hobbes was a proponent of science and a mechanistic view of the world and this was important because this would take government, the founders' "science of politics," out of the realm of morality and/or superstition and make it based on rational principles. So science and the *automata* were good because the state could be seen as value neutral.

But Serling has a more nuanced view of modernity and the mechanistic view. Is science really better than rationality? Is science really better than superstition? Is it better than magic? These are questions Serling considers and for him sometimes the answer is that modernity and the mechanistic view have a flip side as do the overreliance on mechanisms and rationality.

This is the Rousseauian view—the criticism of the overreliance on mechanisms.

This is a theme—the mechanistic idea of humans and the universe—that Serling uses in *The Twilight Zone* where people are seen as *automata* or robots either for evil or good. It is a modern view of the world, but Serling has mixed feelings about modernity as shown in *The Twilight Zone*. His ambivalence about modernity is reflected in his ambivalence about machines and shown in such shows as "A Thing about Machines," "The Bewitchin' Pool" (written by Earl Hamner, Jr.), "A Stop at Willoughby," "The Lateness of the Hour," "Walking Distance," "Living Doll" (by Jerry Sohl and Charles Beaumont), "Uncle Simon" and "In His Image" by Charles Beaumont.

In "Lateness" Serling takes the idea of *automata* literally and to extremes. Again, here we see a wealthy family where there's something sinister beneath the façade.[2] Dr. William Loren and his wife and daughter Jana are in their library before dinner. Dr. Loren is a retired scientist. Everything in the house is "built to perfection."

The Lorens stay in the house and stick to a strict schedule. They are surrounded by servants which are creations of Dr. Loren, what Serling calls a "menagerie for machines." They are robots. Jana accuses them of turning her into an "insulated freak" and becoming dependent on the robots. She wants her freedom and begins packing to leave the mansion, but Dr. Loren gets rid of the servants. Jana is happy and decides to stay but she wonders why there are no pictures of her as a child in the photo albums in the library. She is a robot too, "a machine."

Serling's voiceover is something about the "rat race" and the "neuroses of the twentieth century" and this story has themes of modern day alienation and overreliance on machines and science where Hobbes's idea of *automata* is taken literally. For Hobbes, science was good because if we know human nature we can create a state based on it, but Serling saw the flip side of dependency on it. For Serling the overreliance on machines was part of modernity that he questioned as being commercial and alienating.

The blurring between *automata* and people is also seen in "The After Hours" set in a store with mannequins. Marcia White, a shopper, takes the elevator to the ninth floor to buy a gold thimble. The saleslady is strange and knows her name. She goes to the manager to complain about a dent in the thimble and he tells her there is no ninth floor. She sees the saleslady who waited on her on the ninth floor—she is a mannequin. Marcia goes to rest and is locked in after the store closes on a floor full of mannequins who are calling her. The mannequins come to life. Marcia remembers that she is a mannequin and it was her turn to become a person for a month. Now it's the saleslady's turn—each of the mannequins gets to be a person and then goes back to being a mannequin "a wooden lady with a painted face."

The happy *automata* of Hobbes's *Leviathan* are also pictured in "The Mighty Casey" and "I Sing the Body Electric."[3] "Casey" is the next show in season one after "The After Hours" and is about the Hoboken Zephyrs a baseball team in New Jersey.[4] The manager, Mr. McGarry, hires a new pitcher, Casey, a robot who is the creation of Dr. Stillman.[5]

Casey has extraordinary strength. Dr. Stillman is a creator of robots and tells McGary "once I built a home economist. A marvelous cook. I gained 46 lbs. before I had to dismantle her." He wants Casey to pitch in "the worst ball team" to demonstrate that he can pitch. It works and the Zephyrs win games until Casey is hit on the head and the team doctor sees that Casey has no pulse and that he's a robot. As team physician he tells the Baseball Commission. The owner argues that Casey is human "he's got arms and legs and a face and he talks." But the Baseball Commission says this violates the rules. The commissioner agrees to give Casey a temporary ok if he gets a heart but then he can't pitch because he feels compassion and he doesn't want to strike people out. Dr. Stillman says Casey "hasn't been around long enough to understand competitiveness or drive or ego." Casey decides he wants to go into social work and help people. He is nice.

"The Mighty Casey" plays up the different views of human nature of Hobbes and Rousseau. For Hobbes, humans are egoistic and mechanistic, they move toward their appetites and away from their aversions. They are belligerent and not compassionate but this is good because it makes statecraft value neutral.

For Rousseau, humans are compassionate. They only seem belligerent and egoistic. They are virtuous and their main virtue is compassion. They are not competitive. Casey *before* is Hobbes, Casey *after* is Rousseau.

In "I Sing the Body Electric," written by Ray Bradbury, Hobbes's *automaton* is a robot nanny. A man with three children needs someone to take care of them for "guidance . . . someone around who cares." The boy sees an ad for "I sing the body electric" the motto of Facsimile Ltd "makers of . . . effigies, mimics, mannequins . . . to parents who worry about inadequate nurses . . . who are concerned with the moral and social development of their children." Facsimile Ltd. advertises "we have perfected an electronic data processing system in the shape of an elderly woman." As their father says "sort of a robot." The daughter asks "can they build a machine like a human?"

The family goes to a dark showroom with a mannequin torso in the window where they pick out all the body parts for the facsimile. They even choose a voice. The robot shows up at their house. She holds up her hand and marbles appear. The girl, Anne says "she's not real, she's a machine" but the robot says "this machine can love."

Here we see the contrast between "mechanistic" and "compassion" in Hobbes and Rousseau, but Bradbury brings these together brilliantly here, as Serling does in "The Mighty Casey" and "The Lonely" which combine mechanistic elements with compassion.

The theme of the alienating quality of machines is continued in "The Brain Center at Whipple's" and "The Dummy." In "The Dummy" Jerry Etherson, a ventriloquist, and Willy are a nightclub act. Jerry is convinced that Willy is alive. Jerry switches to another dummy. He locks Willy in a trunk and hears his voice. They fight and Willy wins—he becomes the ventriloquist and Jerry the dummy. The theme of the dummy as alive is continued in "Living Doll" in the fifth season where a doll becomes a murderer because the stepfather of the girl who owns it does not like it.

"A Thing about Machines" is perhaps the most pessimistic of the mechanistic shows in which Mr. Bartlett Finchley, a food writer, is haunted by the world of machines. Finchley lives in a mansion with a swimming pool, two images that Serling uses to represent modernity and affluence that don't necessarily correspond to happiness.

As the show opens we see the TV repairman at Finchley's mansion. He was there before to repair the radio. The repairmen listens to Finchley's complaining and asks "Finchley—what is it with you and machines?" Finchley is exasperated and says "it just so happens that every machine in this house is . . ." The antique clock chimes and he smashes it but it keeps chiming until he hits it with a fireplace poker. Serling comes on Finchley's TV and says "he has no purpose to his life except the day-to-day opportunities to vent his wrath on mechanical contrivances of an age he abhors."

Finchley is a modern day Luddite.[6] He is anti-mechanistic and his rejection of machines is part of the rejection of modernity. He berates his secretary for typing too slowly on that "idiotic machine" the typewriter and prefers the quill pen of Thomas Jefferson. His secretary, Miss Rogers, quits. Finchley panics because she is his only connection to people. He's lonely and asks her to stay. The machines are closing in on him. At last Finchley drinks himself into a stupor and when he wakes up the clock is chiming, the typewriter is typing "Get out of here Finchley" and he smashes the TV. As he runs upstairs the electric razor comes down the stairs like a snake—he rushes outside and the car chases him into the swimming pool, the headlights staring at him like eyes. Finchley has been avenged by the triumph of the machines he hates and drowned in his own pool—symbol of success.

The theme of the modern age represented by machines turning on people is in many of the fifth season shows, including "The Brain Center at Whipple's" which takes a Marxian view of modern capitalism where machines not only turn on you but they throw you out of (not a window but) a job.[7] The year is 1967 and the WV Whipple Manufacturing Corporation shows workers on an assembly line. They have a machine that eliminates jobs and the X109B14 modified transistorized machine will make the production totally automatic. Mr. Whipple has a habit of twirling his watch fob, and a habit of seeking to put machines in the jobs of workers.

Mr. Hanley is the plant manager and he doesn't like that it puts "a lot of men out of work." Whipple explains "that, unfortunately, is progress." Whipple talks to the machine as if it's a person. Mr. Hanley says "why are you so eager to replace men with machines? Did it ever occur to you that you might be trading efficiency for pride? Pride, craftsmanship. What a man feels when he makes something." Hanley's soliloquy could come straight from the *Communist Manifesto*: "modern industry has converted the little workshop of the patriarchal master into the great factory of the individual capitalist."

A workman looking at the machine says to Mr. Hanley "ever notice how it looks like it had a face? An ugly face, a miserable ugly face." This is the ugly face of modern capitalism where profits are king and pride is not, and where the modern and mechanized are exalted rather than the creative workers: "owing to the . . . use of machinery the work of the proletarians" has no individual character and no "charm for the workman" and the worker "becomes an appendage of the machine."[8] In fact, the workers are "enslaved by the machine, by the over-looker."[9]

The next scene is a man in a bar across the street telling the bartender his hands are "obsolete"—again, reference from Marx. The man, Dickerson, is drunk. He's worked there for 30 years. Mr. Whipple explains the machine "gets no wrinkles, no arthritis . . . 2 of those machines replace 114 men a day . . . and that is worth considerably more than you." Again, no Rousseauian compassion, as Rousseau talked about "man and his machines" in the "Discourse on the Origin of Inequality" as "the first yoke . . . For, besides continuing thus to enervate both body and mind, these conveniences lost with use almost all their power to please . . . till the want of them became far more disagreeable than the possession of them had been pleasant." Mr. Dickerson replies "I'm a man . . . and that makes me better than that hunk of metal, ya hear me?" He takes a crowbar to the machine and it sparks and sets on fire, Mr. Dickerson collapses.

Mr. Whipple gets a machine that replaces Hanley. Hanley slaps him for his lack of compassion. All the people quit or are fired. The machines start to go off at the same time. Finally, Whipple himself comes into the bar. Hanley is there. Whipple asks him how retirement is going and says "a man should have time for leisure when he grows older." The Board of Directors makes him step down. He is replaced with a machine that twirls its keychain like Whipple. "It's not fair, Hanley, it's not fair—a man has value, a man has worth" and they show the robot twirling the keychain. Whipple comes to the Rousseauian Marxian idea of human value only after *his* job is offered to a machine.

Serling uses the theme of *automata*, or robots, to emphasize science and modernity. The theme figures into episodes in season five including "Steel," "Living Doll," "The Old Man in the Cave," "Uncle Simon," "Number Twelve Looks Just Like You," "From Agnes with love," "Caesar and Me," and "The Brain Center at Whipple's." These *Twilight Zones* were written between 1963–1964 during the Johnson administration, which made science, including space travel, one of its most important themes. Yet, Serling seems not to approve of the effects of modernity and automation.

In "Steel," written by Richard Matheson, robot beats man in a boxing match. It's 1974 and a 1968 law has outlawed prize fighting. Robots or, as Serling says, androids or "an automaton resembling a human being" replaced men in the boxing ring. Two guys have a fighting robot "Maxo" who is falling apart—his wheels are coming off.

Maxo's manager is "Steel" Kelly (Lee Marvin) who was a boxer before the 1968 law. He and his friend check Maxo's batteries and circuits where they can program him, a spring comes out and they cannot use the robot. Steel decides that he will pretend to be the robot and go in the ring against the other robot. They must deliver a fight to get paid and nobody knows what Maxo looks like so Steel can pretend to be a robot, the classic "man against machine" theme.

Lee Marvin pretends to be the robot, but the real robot wins. Lee Marvin collapses. Serling's voiceover says: "no matter what the future brings man's capacity to rise to the occasion will remain unaltered. His potential for tenacity and optimism continues as always . . . for which three cheers and a unanimous decision rendered from the Twilight Zone." This, in spite of the fact that the robot won, and civilization will now be run by robots and *automata* rather than men.

"Caesar and Me" written by Adele T. Strassfield is the same message—robots rule. This is about a man, Mr. West, played by Jackie Cooper, who is a ventriloquist and has an act "Little Caesar and Jonathan." The dummy talks and is "a small splinter with large ideas" and "a wooden tyrant with a mind and a voice of his own."

A little girl named Susan thinks that Caesar can really talk. The dummy is the ambitious one. West is the loser—Caesar wears a diamond horseshoe tie pin and a pinkie ring. West says he just wants enough money "to buy some food and pay the rent" and Caesar says "is that all you want out of life? You're a clod."

The dummy says "I've had enough" and convinces West to rob a deli to pay the rent. He says "you act penny ante because you think penny ante." Susan breaks into West's room and tells the dummy she knows he he can talk. Next they rob a theater. Susan listens at their door and hears them discussing the burglary. She calls the police. They take West to the station (he works for the dummy) and leave Caesar who says to Susan "you're a hip little kid. I like you." He convinces her to run away and do the act with him in New York. Serling's voiceover: "a . . . dummy in the shape of a man."

"In His Image," written by Charles Beaumont, is Hobbes' *automata*—about a man named Alan Talbot who works with computers. When he drives to his hometown with his fiancé, Jessica, he tells her "in sparking circles I was known as the human electrode." His hometown is "Coeurville" reminiscent of The Tin Man in *The Wizard of Oz* but when he's there everything is different from the way he remembers it. He goes to his Aunt Mildred's house but she doesn't live there. He goes to the coffee shop at the hotel but there's no coffee shop there.

Meanwhile, Alan has episodes that sound like static. He works at the University of Coeurville—which isn't there. He is like Rip Van Winkle and 20 years have gone by since he was there. Jessica says "there's a rational explanation for this" and in the Hobbesian world of *automata* there is—Alan Talbot is a robot.

Alan is a robot twin created in the image of the scientist who made him. He pulls back his skin and you can see the wires in his hand, a technique also used in "The Lonely." His alter ego, Walter Ryder, says "you're a machine, Alan, a mechanical device." Walter tells him that this was his dream "I thought about one thing . . . a perfect artificial man, not a robot, a duplicate of a human being." Walter takes Alan to his lab where there are other Alan Talbot mechanical men. Walter goes to Jessica's house as Alan and she asks if he wants some eggs saying "they're guaranteed to make a new man out of you" not realizing that she is now talking to a man rather than a robot.

An automaton in the guise of a computer takes over in "From Agnes with Love," written by Bernard Shoenfeld. Here, a computer falls in love with a man, James Elwood, and this is the flip side of a man falling in love with a machine in "The Lonely." The computer manipulates the scientist and tells him how to behave with a girlfriend so that he alienates her. The computer takes over his life and makes him quit his job by driving him crazy. The computers are taking over contemporary society and if we rely on them they will lead us astray and away from people connections.

Robots and computers can pretend to be people but in reality the over mechanized society leads to loneliness and alienation, as Agnes ruins Jim's relationship and he ends up alienated, driven mad, and alone.

The idea of the *automata* and the "Artificial Man" are right out of Hobbes. But so are the theme of alienation and mechanization. Alan says that Jessica is "pretty, intelligent and lonely" the same theme in "The Lonely" where robots lead us astray and alienate us, only here he's the robot not her. Fascism figures in with the mechanistic element of modernity, the idea that the leader gets his message out via use of the media, and the idea that he is always watching you.

The Bandstand and the Swimming Pool

Perhaps one of the best known shows that depicts the tensions of modernity, and Serling's antipathy to it, is "A Stop at Willoughby" about a harried New York businessman who invents an imaginary and bucolic nineteenth-century town as he commutes back to his house in Westport, Connecticut, a place with which Serling was familiar.

Gart Williams works in the competitive world of New York City advertising where his boss pressures him to compete in the rat race for status and money. Gart does not like the pace of life and prefers a small town atmosphere and the image of Huckleberry Finn. Gart's wife, Janie, is a social climber who also pushes him to succeed in a materialistic world.

Gart needs an escape and he invents one in the town of Willoughby. When he commutes home at night to Westport it's winter and it's snowing. The cold represents not only the weather outside, but also how he feels inside—cold, isolated and alone in a world that values only money and status, and the coldness of the big city. Gart dreams he is in a train that goes to the nineteenth century town where the sun is shining and it's summer of 1888—before the World Wars, a time of peace, where kids with straw hats walk by carrying fish on poles and where the bandstand symbolizes the bucolic idealic small town of Serling's youth where people live "full measure" and community is prized over individualism. This is in contrast to Westport where it's snowing and where Gart needs to go for a drink as soon as he gets home, even though he obviously has stomach trouble.

Gart's wife is disgusted that he would be happy with an ice wagon and a horse drawn carriage. The bandstand, where the community can come to hear concerts, figures prominently as the symbol of community and tranquility and peace and harmony before the modern day rat race promoted individualism at the expense of community. The bandstand is the first thing Gart sees when he steps off the train in Willoughby—he throws away his briefcase on the train, a gesture of rejection of the rat race in favor of the community of Willoughby. Remember—this is the community, not the state. We do not see any agents of the state, just people having a good time, fishing and enjoying the band concert. For Serling, this scene represents the upstate New York of his youth that he visited during summers and the community's warmth that he remembered.

Willoughby's bandstand, and the bandshell as a symbol, is an oasis within an oasis, a sanctuary within a sanctuary. The bandstand is a creation of traditional society and symbolizes a place where the community could get together and listen to a band at leisure. It symbolizes community, leisure and a simpler and happy time before the World Wars, the nuclear bomb, and competition threatened social ties that hold people together. In *Democracy in America*, Volume 2, Book 2, chapter 2, Tocqueville said traditional society "had made a chain of all the members of the community . . . democracy breaks that chain and severs every link of it." Though the nineteenth century was a time of the Industrial Revolution, it wasn't a place of competition and the rat race we associate with post WWII America.

The two views of nineteenth versus twentieth-century America can be seen in Gart and his wife, Janie—he symbolizes the bucolic Huck Finn of the nineteenth century and she the status seeker who tries to keep up with the Joneses in suburban Westport. She is a snob, but there is no need for snobbery in Willoughby. Serling had seen WWII and, as a pacificist, used the bandstand to hark back to the time of the ice wagon and horse drawn carriage. Gart could indeed be happy with an ice wagon, horse drawn carriage and bandstand as his wife notes disapprovingly. In "A Short Drink from a Certain Fountain" Flora, the materialistic wife, says "we'll do something really wild—like go to a band conert in the park." Serling's view of a snob is someone who disparages a bandstand!

The bandstand is a reference to Binghamton and, according to Gordon Sander, references to Binghamton and towns like it are a theme in both "A Stop at Willoughby" and "Walking Distance."[10] Sander describes Binghamton as a place with "verdant parks filled with gazebos and carousels"[11] where "band concerts were perhaps its most popular . . . form of culture"[12] and ". . . to young Rod Serling, it was . . . Willoughby."[13]

In "Walking Distance" Martin Sloan goes to his home town—he is impatient as he honks his horn at the gas station when his car breaks down. He, like Gart Williams, is an ad executive in New York and, like Gart Williams, fed up with it. He escapes to the town of Homewood, his hometown, and like Gart he walks into the past. But now it's his past.

Martin walks to the park where you see the ice cream man and a lady who rhapsodizes on "band concerts." The bandstand where he carved his name is prominent. He sees himself carving his name on the post of the bandstand. Martin runs away—the young Martin runs away, as Martin's youth has escaped (a theme that is seen in other *Twilight Zones* such as "The Incredible World of "Horace Ford"). Martin goes to his house and tells his father that he wants to stop running in the rat race, the Hobbesian "race of life" which has, according to Hobbes, "no other purpose" than to win. There is a carousel in the park next to the bandstand, also a symbol of the bucolic small town.

Perhaps Serling's strongest statement against the twentieth century is "No Time Like the Past" in which Paul Driscoll characterizes the twentieth century as a "cesspool" with a race of miserable men with "hatreds . . . prejudices . . . and violence." He decries the "strontium 90" in the milk and decides he wants to go back to alter history, but when he realizes he can't alter history he asks a scientist, Harvey, to send him back to a place with "band concerts" where there are no bombs, fallout, radioactivity or other evils of the twentieth century which he calls "bedlam." Serling's romance with the nineteenth century, and his disillusionment with modernity, come out where the past is called "inviolate" and the bandstand becomes a sanctuary for the two heroes, Paul and Abby. For him, the nineteenth century and traditional society are so pure and untouched by atom bombs and World Wars and the bandstand and horse drawn carriage symbolize this purity, as in "A Stop at Willoughby." There's no rat race, as in Hollywood or Westport, and Paul can chat with a man practicing for a band concert in the gazebo.

When Paul goes back to Homeville, Indiana, the first thing we see is the town square with the bandstand. It is summer, 1881—just like in Willoughby, before the World Wars. Abby, a schoolteacher the landlady says is "real moral" symbolizes this purity, as does her name—as in an abbey. Paul symbolizes St. Paul. The past is sacred and she is abbey and he is St. Paul and the gazebo is holy, a shrine to the past. Here, perhaps more than anywhere else, the bandstand is featured most prominently as a symbol of peace. When we see Abby, and every time the school where she teaches is shown, there is a horse drawn carriage, a symbol of the bucolic nineteenth century before the modern world.

This is the horse drawn carriage that Gart's wife, Janie, speaks of with disgust in "A Stop at Willoughby." The carriage is always in the background here, as is the gazebo.

As Paul muses against the twentieth century and "nuclear fallout, Indochina, the Berlin Wall" he feels safe in his nineteenth-century room at the boarding house saying "I never heard of you." He looks out his window at the gazebo and says "It's summer . . . there's going to be a band concert in a couple of days. . . ." These things, the band concert and gazebo, make him feel safe, just as they made Gart feel safe and Janie feel disgusted in "Willoughby." There are no evils of the modern age, but even here President Garfield is shot and even here the bigoted man at the boarding house calls for war.

"No Time Like the Past" is Serling's romantic view of the past including his own past in upstate New York—where he enjoyed carousels, ice cream and summer nights.[14] For him, the past is contrasted to the modern world of technology, wars and bombs, mechanization, automation, and alienation. According to his daughter, he liked the idea of going back to a simpler place and time, like a Huck Finn-inspired town.[15] A small town in the nineteenth century is, for Serling, a place like Willoughby where a man can do things "full measure."

The whole idea of the merry-go-round which figures prominently in "Walking Distance," according to the Stoic philosopher Epictetus, is that it goes around once and we should think of it like a banquet: "Think of your life as if it were a banquet where you would behave graciously. When dishes are passed to you extend your hand and help yourself to a moderate portion. If a dish should pass you by, enjoy what is already on your plate. Or if the dish hasn't been passed to you yet, patiently wait your turn."[16] This is the idea expressed in "Walking Distance"—this is *his* summer, you had your summer.

In contrast to the bandstand is the swimming pool, the symbol of pretentiousness and snobbery that represents the materialistic values that run counter to community. In "The Bewitchin' Pool," written by Earl Hamner Jr., the scene is set in the backyard of a rich suburban couple featuring a glittering swimming pool, the message being that all that glitters is not gold. Two children, Jeb and Scout Sherwood, vanish into the pool—it's a means of escape, just like the car was a means of escape for Mr. Sloan in "Walking Distance" and the train a means of escape for Mr. Williams in "A Stop at Willoughby." But the pool is also a symbol of false opulence and values, a materialistic symbol of status that Serling felt was phony. For him, this is a façade.

Just like Gart Williams, Mr. Sherwood, the owner the swimming pool which the children use to escape, hits the bar when he gets home. Scout, one of the children, looks at the pool but sees a river and imagines them floating on a raft like Tom Sawyer, as opposed to Janie Williams' disparaging Huckleberry Finn.

The pool is the vehicle that takes them to the past, just like the car takes Mr. Sloan and the train takes Mr. Williams. They swim out of the twentieth century and into the nineteenth-century town of "Aunt T" who is in the kitchen baking. She is old fashioned, and presides over the homely arts as contrasted to Janie Williams and Mrs. Sherwood who is modern and wants a career outside the home.

Aunt T is weaving and baking cakes—she is traditional. The children, like Gart Williams, stay in the nineteenth century and reject the phonies, snobs and swimming pools of the twentieth century, preferring the swimming hole of Huck and Tom Sawyer to "wet entertainment for the well to do."

The image of the swimming pool figures prominently in other *Twilight Zones*, the "Queen of the Nile" and "A Thing About Machines." In both stories the scene opens with an image of the swimming pool, a symbol of the façade of civility for Serling, but here the pools are a symbol of downright evil. In "Queen of the Nile" the glimmering swimming pool is where we first see Pamela, the film star. The pool is part of the façade of success which belies the phoniness of the owner. This fits Hollywood—a twentieth century town of phoniness and image.

Serling himself had a pool when he moved to Hollywood. According to Sander "the house had . . . nine bedrooms, a tennis court, Japanese gardens, and, of course, a swimming pool . . . Serling felt guilty about leaving New York for Los Angeles—the land of mink swimming pools, as he used to kiddingly call it around that time."[17] But according to Serling Hollywood was a nice place for a grapefruit.[18]

Serling's pool, according to Sander, was "the very same sort of pool that Serling and his friends . . . used to nervously joke about when they 'sold out' and left New York" and this was "the metaphor . . . used for spiritual corruption in his autobiographical study of the hazards of Hollywood-style TV writing, 'The Velvet Alley.'"[19] In a 1959 interview with Mike Wallace, Serling talked about "The Velvet Alley" and "preoccupation with status—with the symbols of status, with the heated swimming pool. . . ."[20] In talking about Serling's careeer, Mike Wallace said his success took him "from a trailer home to a hacienda in Hollywood complete with swimming pool. . . ."[21]

The image of the pool is not only one of phoniness and pretentiousness but it is sinister and the residents of homes with pools in *The Twilight Zone* are caught up in the competitive and superficial Hobbesian "race of life"—in Pamela's case, in "Queen of the Nile" the race to stay beautiful at the expense of others. For her, the swimming pool symbolizes the fountain of youth which she achieves in a sinister way.

In the "Ring-a-Ding Girl," written by Earl Hamner, Jr., the scene opens with a swimming pool at the Hollywood home of movie star Bunny Blake—

but she rejects Hollywood and the swimming pool and goes back to her hometown of Howardville to save the community. She doesn't like Hollywood, she throws her mink coat on the floor, and wonders why she left. She is a rich person in *The Twilight Zone* who likes the bandstand not the swimming pool.

Likewise, in "A Thing About Machines" the scene opens with the pool at the mansion of Mr. Bartlett Finchley a pretentious misanthrope. If the bandstand is a symbol of community and commonweal, the pool is a symbol of isolation and alienation of the haughty rich from their fellows, which is symbolized when Finchley shoos away his nosy neighbors. Finchley, Williams, The Sherwoods and Pamela have material things but they are isolated and alienated by the competition of the rat race which is symbolized by the pool—a symbol of success just as the gazebo is a symbol of happiness.

Fascism and Dictatorship

> As I would not be a *slave*, so I would not be a *master*. This expresses my idea of democracy.
>
> —Abraham Lincoln, in *The Collected Works of Abraham Lincoln*
> by Roy P. Basler

Serling is anti-Fascist and against all prejudice and these are the themes in such shows as "On Thursday We Leave for Home," "He's Alive," and others. Serling had a strong individualistic steak, and a strong respect for human rights and individual liberties which made him reject collectivistic governments and he "put much thought into the issues of tyranny and the misuse of power."[22] He enlisted in WWII as a teenager to join the effort against fascism and the strong anti-fascist streak comes across in a variety of ways and in a variety of shows, including "It's A Good Life," "The Obsolete Man," "The Eye of the Beholder," etc. Serling's speech at Moorpark College in December 1968 created controversy over his refusal to sign a loyalty oath to speak. In his speech at the College he said, "Fascists and Communists . . . distrust . . . their own people" and force them to sign loyalty oaths.

"He's Alive" deals with the theme of fascism because of its references to Hitler and the Nazis, but Serling points out that the idea of fascism owes a great debt to its racist content, that fascism and racism go together and that you cannot have fascism without racism.

Pete is a young Nazi, a fascist preaching hatred of Jews, Blacks, Asians and Catholics who, Serling says, looks for wisdom in the sewer. He tries to rouse a group to hatred but the crowd throws tomatoes at him. He goes to the house of his friend Ernst, who is Jewish and whom he has known since he was young, and is visited by a shadowy figure. Ernst says that Pete peddles hate and he should know—he was in Dachau, the Nazi concentration camp. Ernst says that the Nazis started with young men on the street propagandizing people but he thinks of Pete as a troubled kid trying to look for his identity.

A stranger comes to Pete in the middle of the night to tell him how to sway the mob so they won't throw tomatoes at him. Pete listens to the stranger, and rants about the "minorities" with a poster of Hitler in back while preaching for a white America. He also implies that the Jews gave the bomb to the Russians. Pete's idea of freedom is to get rid of "foreigners" and "mongrels." Just as the stranger said, this works and Pete has a big rally with a lot of people. The Jewish landlord wants the rent money—and he gets it, from the shadowy figure.

The stranger, a hallucination, tells Pete they need a martyr and Pete asks Frank to kill Nick, another Nazi, to martyr him. This time when Pete preaches Ernst is in the audience contradicting him. Ernst says fascists are neurotics who need praise. Pete hits him. Fascists only know violence, though Ernst says bullets don't stop ideas. The shadowy figure, claiming he "invented darkness" steps out of the darkness—it's Hitler who says even though he sent "them" to the ovens there were always some to "point a finger" like Ernst. He tells Pete to kill Ernst and Pete goes to Ernst's room and shoots him.

Serling's voiceover makes it clear that fascism runs on racism and prejudice. The "He" refers to Hitler and we can see the shadow of Hitler wherever there is hatred, racism and bigotry or assaults on people because of their race, religion, creed or color.

In "On Thursday We Leave for Home" some Earthlings have been stranded on another planet for 30 years, they left the Earth looking for a place with no war or fear. The planet has two suns and the people must wear hats and sweat constantly because of the heat. They live in a cave, away from the suns, and wear khaki uniforms. The scenery is barren and people start to commit suicide.

The colony in "On Thursday" is ruled by a Captain William Benteen, who has been their dictator. Benteen explains that his rules kept the group from degenerating into a "free for all" and the state of nature where there is no government. So Benteen takes over being all three branches and governing the people. He is the state. He leads them and takes care of them like a flock of sheep after a meteor shower—the paternalistic state. He caters to the group and tells the children stories about Earth.

A ship comes from Earth to rescue them with Colonel Sloane. Benteen asks Sloane if there are still wars on Earth. He says yes, but by some "miracle" they didn't have a hydrogen war. Colonel Sloane keeps calling him "Mr. Benteen" and Benteen keeps correcting him to say "Captain Benteen" showing his love of complete power.

When the group is rescued the people show less interest in Benteen—now they listen to Colonel Sloane. When Sloane convenes a meeting about Earth Benteen wants to conduct the meeting. Colonel Sloane wants to play baseball but Benteen says it's too hot and "in this place, I'm in command." Benteen couches his dictates in "concern" for the people and calls them "his people." Sloane says that the group will scatter over the 50 states, but Benteen wants the group to go together as a community. Dictators are collectivists because they do not want individualism which threatens their total control.

One of the group, Al, says he doesn't want to stay together but Benteen says "together . . . that's the word . . . say it with me . . . together" which is the expression of organic collectivist community where there is one idea, one religion, one leader. Sloane says that now it's time for the group to be individuals and, even though there is war and prejudice on Earth it has freedom and "let's every man be his own master. There won't be any captain Benteens." Rather than "Earth" perhaps Serling meant "America" has freedom because there are dictators on Earth, but not in America with a Constitution, freedom of speech, press and religion. They vote, and even the child votes to go to Earth.

Benteen, a dictator, refuses to be rescued—he would rather stay alone on an empty planet than go back to being a citizen because the one thing that dictators will not stand is being powerless. He tries to break Sloane's spaceship, runs away and convenes an empty gathering in the cave but even he decides that he'd rather have freedom. Serling's voiceover says that Benteen "could lead" and then had to dictate because it became his identity. The message of "On Thursday" is that people want freedom given the choice of freedom and dictatorship. Serling rejects the idea of modern, collectivist societies ruled by dictators, in favor of freedom and the individual.

"Eye of the Beholder" is about a fascist state where not only do people have to think the same, act the same, have "a single purpose, a single norm, a single approach, a single entity of people, a single virtue" but they have to look the same too. People who look different are sent by the state, where ugliness as defined by the state is a crime, to a colony with others who have committed the same "crime" because according to this totalitarian society "differences weaken us." This idea that differences weaken us is anti-American because Americans believe that diversity and differences of opinion, the marketplace of ideas and freedom to express them, is America's strength and where it gets its greatness.

"The Mirror," first aired in 1961, is also about a dictator and is Serling's "commentary on Fidel Castro, two years after Castro assumed power and a year before the Cuban Missile Crisis."[23] The dictator is the most hated man, and he even hates himself. Tyranny is hard to maintain, because in a tyranny there is no legitimacy and in a regime where there is no legitimacy there are always people scheming against the regime and against the dictator. A dictator in "The Mirror" says there is power that comes with dictatorship but also fear "of assassination, fear of disloyalty, fear of rebellion. . . ."

Serling's dictator in "The Mirror" personifies this hatred of dictatorship. This show was aired in 1961 during the beginning of the presidency of John F. Kennedy who made three things the hallmark of his presidency: going to the moon, civil rights, and anti-communism. Not only was John F. Kennedy anti-Communist, but his brother, Robert Kennedy, worked with Roy Cohn and Joseph McCarthy on the anti-communist hearings. Serling was a proponent of free-speech and no doubt did not like the effect that the McCarthy hearings had on Hollywood.[24] Nonetheless, he is also anti-totalitarianism and anti-collectivistic, whether it be from the left or the right.

The scene of "The Mirror" is set in one room in a palace. A Fidel Castro-style Latin American dictator, Ramos Clemente played by Peter Falk, stands out on his balcony waving to the crowds and toasts "to the revolution." Another dictator says to Clemente "we care for no one but ourselves."

A mirror was given to the former dictator and if you look in it you see your assassins. Clemente tells his henchmen to shoot all the prisoners because trials are not convenient. He looks in the mirror and his henchman is pointing a gun at him. Clemente throws him out the window. He sees other henchmen in the mirror, other assassins. The remaining henchman, Christo, says that dictators have no friends only enemies and competitors or followers. Clemente thinks that Christo is a follower until Christo has more power than Clemente so Clemente kills Christo.

A priest comes to see Clemente to tell him that the people "are appalled" at all the executions—as Machiavelli says it cannot be called virtue to kill fellow citizens and a prince cannot achieve honor this way. But the dictator is not a prince, he is a dictator which, as Aristotle says, is a perversion of a prince and does not care about honor. Clemente tells him if they don't like it "let them go into caves."

Clemente tells the priest that he's frightened and asks why he has so many enemies. Tomas tells him "this is the story of all tyrants. They have but one real enemy" and that is themselves. Just like in "The Monsters are due on Maple St." they pick the worst enemy they know and it's always themselves. People, like dictators, tyrannize themselves. Clemente looks in the mirror, sees himself, breaks the mirror and shoots himself.

Anthony Fremont also wants "a single approach, a single virtue" in "It's A Good Life." Here, Anthony is the dictator. Even though he is only a little boy his powers make him hold an entire town in fear which is the way dictators, fascist and totalitarian governments control their people. If he doesn't like singing, they don't like it. If he doesn't like dancing, they don't like it. But, as Christo says in "The Mirror," dictators have no friends only enemies who pretend to be followers.

Any state that makes the individual "obsolete" is a fascist state, the theme in "The Obsolete Man." Here is a futuristic society where books are banned and librarians, such as Mr. Wordsworth, played by Burgess Meredith in much the same role he played in "Time Enough at Last," are "obsolete." This is a fascist society, where the goal is the elimination of individual freedom including freedom of speech and of the press and of books. Here, the executions are televised because of the "educational" value.

In "Deaths-Head Revisited" Serling shows Nazis for what they are—bloodthirsty and without any conscience. Here Lutze, a former SS Captain, is sentenced to go mad by the ghosts of Dachau. Serling says that Dachau is standing as a monument to fascism so that people may not repeat the crimes of the twentieth century and we should remember this "not only in the Twilight Zone" but everywhere. This is one of the few shows that doesn't end with the words "Twilight Zone" because Serling wanted to make a political statement, as with "I Am the Night—Color Me Black."

Serling enlisted in World War II which was a war against Nazis and fascism. He used *The Twilight Zone* to highlight, perhaps more than any other theme, the collectivist political theories, including fascism, he considered to be the most negative aspects of modernity.

In "The Little People" astronaut Peter Craig wants to order people around. He and astronaut William Fletcher land on a planet with a civilization of miniature people that he wants to dictate to. The little people are scared, Craig can step on them, and he does. Craig does not want to go back to Earth with William Fletcher—the little people have built a monument to him so he won't step on them. Craig is giddy with his power until another spaceship comes to the planet with astronauts who are giants. Now Craig is "little," now they step on him. The little people pull down the statue they erected to him.

As in "The Mirror," nobody likes a dictator, including Serling.

The Cold War

The Cold War, symbolized by the Cuban Missile crisis of 1962, was the theme of several shows including "The Jeopardy Room" and "The Whole Truth." Most of *The Twilight Zone* shows were originally aired between 1959–1964, roughly corresponding to the presidency of John F. Kennedy who, we might assume from "The Whole Truth," Serling admired.[25]

It wasn't just in *The Twilight Zone* that people were building bomb shelters—just ask anyone in suburbia from Long Island to Wisconsin, where people in the 1950s were building bomb shelters and stocking them with canned food and provisions for a nuclear war. This was the atmosphere in America of the 1950s, the Cold War with the Soviet Union. America had the atom bomb, but so did the Soviets. America wanted to put astronauts into space, and so did the Soviets. So there was a space race and a weapons race that created an atmosphere of fear about the atom bomb and its effects. Certainly, after Hiroshima and Nagasaki nobody wanted to see the bomb used again, a theme in "No Time Like the Past" where Paul Driscoll goes back in time to try to tell the people of Hiroshima that the bomb is going to be dropped.

The Cold War with the Soviets, including the execution of the Rosenbergs for espionage, culminated in the Cuban Missile Crisis of 1962 where Kennedy went eye to eye with the Soviets and the United States was on the brink of nuclear war. Only because of Kennedy's brilliant diplomacy, and that of the group of people who advised him, were we able to avoid an atomic war but in the wake of the Missile Crisis everyone was more aware of how close we came to nuclear war and how important it was to avoid it.

Tensions with Cuba and the Soviet Union were high and this theme is reflected in *The Twilight Zone*. "The Jeopardy Room" is a clear reference to Soviet spies and the Cold War. Here, all the action takes place in one room with Major Ivan Kuchenko, a Soviet spy who wants to leave and go to the west. There is a bed and a telephone in the room and two counter Russian spies are spying on him. A man knocks on the door and says that Siberia must have been cold enough to motivate Kuchenko to leave his "native country."

Kuchenko was a political prisoner who escaped from Siberia after 12 years and is in a "neutral country" that he is trying to leave for "a western nation" presumably America. Kuchenko thinks he is being spied on by Soviet counter spies. When he is asked by whom he tells the Commissar to look in the mirror. Because he is a former military member they cannot let him go to a western country.

The Soviet Commissar, Vassiloff, drugs Kuchenko with wine and leaves a tape recorder in his room with a tape that says an object in the room is "booby trapped" and he could be blown up unless he can defuse the trap. He is free to go if he can defuse the trap. If he can't defuse the trap he will be shot. The telephone is booby trapped. If he answers the phone when it rings it will blow up. When there are ten minutes left the phone rings, but he doesn't answer it. Instead, he runs out of the room. The Commissar says it's ok, that he'll get him anyway. Now the Commissar's phone rings and Boris, a counter spy, picks it up and it blows up. Kuchenko is at the airport—they announce his flight leaving for New York "via Belgrade, Rome, London." Serling's voiceover says that Major Ivan Kuchenko is on his way to freedom and Commissar Vassiloff isn't, because the Commissar forgot that there are "two parties on the line" and in a battle of wits power goes with those who stand their ground and have more "artistry."

"To Serve Man" also has references to the Cold War when the Soviet representative to the United Nations assumes that the Kanamits from outer space have ulterior motives. The Kanamit also says he will introduce a missile shield or a "force field" to shield each nation with a wall against missiles and bombs. This anticipates the Strategic Defense Initiative, Ronald Reagan's vision, also known as the missile shield "star wars" that would protect America.

"The Shelter" shows the tense relations between America and the Soviet Union, when neighbors believe that aliens are landing on Earth and they all try to take shelter with their neighbor, Dr. Stockton, in his bomb shelter. The only trouble is they cannot all fit, and become a mob as they try to ram down the door of the shelter. The point is that people become a mob when resources, such as shelter, food and water are scarce—but also, that the neighbor with the shelter, the physician, is the only one with the foresight to build it. Here, the "aliens" are substitutes for "Soviets."

The game of cat and mouse played by America and the Soviet Union is parodied in "The Whole Truth," about a used car dealer and a car that makes its owners tell the truth.

Mr. Harvey Hunnicut is a used car salesman and a man brings in an old fashioned Model A car and puts a sign on it that says "like new." He tells Mr. Hunnicut the car is haunted. When Hunnicut asks how it's haunted the man says "you'll find out."

Mr. Hunnicut is now telling the truth. He goes to a couple looking at a car and tells them that it's not worth buying and that nothing in his lot is worth buying. He says that he's got "more lemons" than a "fruit grower." He doesn't just tell the truth about the car—he tells his employee that the car makes people tell the truth. He has to get rid of the car because as long as he has the car he has to tell the truth and he can't sell cars that way! His employee makes signs for the cars that say "not dependable" and "not ready to go."

One day a politician admires the Model A and Hunnicut tells him it's not only a lemon but haunted because the owner of the car must tell the truth. The politician walks away, and tells Hunnicut that he couldn't buy the car because he wouldn't be able to make political speeches or run a campaign, which gives us some idea of what Serling thought of politicians. They point to a picture in the newspaper and agree that they should try to get the person in the picture to tell the truth.

In the next scene a black Cadillac rolls up and a man is negotiating for the Model A for his boss who is in the car. They buy the car for $25 American dollars. The boss in the car is Nikita Khrushchev and Hunnicut quickly makes a call to "Jack Kennedy" because he has news that affects "foreign policy." Khrushchev and his driver drive away in the car.

"The Whole Truth" is Serling's wish that the Soviets would tell the truth so John F. Kennedy could negotiate with them. Unfortunately, this would not come true until the presidency of Ronald Reagan (who said "trust but verify") and later the fall of Soviet communism, which Kennedy's strong stand helped achieve.

"Four O'clock," written by Serling based on a short story by Price Day, also has a Cold War theme that harks to McCarthyism with Mr. Crangle going through lists to see who is a "Communist."

Oliver Crangle calls employers to tell them that their employees are "communists" and "subversives" and that at "four o'clock" there will be an end to "immorality" and the "evil people" will be two feet tall. Crangle tries to take the law into his own hands to judge who is good and who is a subversive. A doctor's wife comes to see Crangle to ask why he is harassing her husband and Crangle says he will not put up with evil—"Communists, subversives, thieves" all the while his parrot is perched on a window sill.

Crangle is like Joseph McCarthy, seeing who is a subversive and who is not. He has a copy of the Gettysburg Address on the wall and he crosses out "all men are created equal." He tries to call Washington but thinks that "the reds are in control" in Washington. An FBI agent, Mr. Hall, visits him and asks Crangle if he has had "psychiatric care" and Crangle says that when he shrinks the "evil people" they'll need more jails for the Communists. Like Tom Paine, Mr. Hall says that, "in America, the law is king."[26]

Prejudice

Prejudice was an important theme for Serling, throughout his career fighting Nazis in World War II and also in *The Twilight Zone*. Some of the shows deal explicitly with prejudice, such as "Dust," "The Gift," "He's Alive," and others such as "The Shelter," "The Monsters are due on Maple Street," "No Time Like the Past," "The Encounter," and "A Quality of Mercy" also deal with the theme. Serling hated bigotry and "prejudice" which, he said, "I abhor more than anything in the world."[27] In his 1968 speech at Moorpark College in California he spoke of African-American girls "bombed to pieces in a Birmingham church" and "three young civil rights workers . . . slaughtered in Mississippi" and decried Senator Strom Thurmond's opposition to anti-lynching legislation.

In "The Shelter," neighbors of a doctor try to cram into his bomb shelter when they think that an alien landing is imminent. They try to outdo each other to get into the shelter and quickly start acting like a mob, where they had all been friendly neighbors at a party. Frank, a neighbor, says that "foreigners" are "pushy" and "grabby" referring to Marty, as they fight to get into the shelter. Even among friends we encounter hatred and prejudice which, according to Serling is the "evil of our time" and "all other evils grow" from it.[28]

When it was considered too controversial to use African-Americans, Serling frequently used Mexican players.[29] In "Dust," Sykes, the peddler, is bigoted against Mexicans and accuses the sheriff of being too nice to foreigners. In "The Gift" we see intergalactic prejudice as people in Mexico, who are now the bigots, segregate and kill an alien from another planet who brought them a gift. Because of their bigotry, they never receive it. In "On Thursday We Leave for Home" Colonel Sloane says that on Earth there is still prejudice.

The Nazi show "He's Alive" is about fascism, but it is also about bigotry and prejudice. Pete preaches hatred against Jews, Blacks, Asians and Catholics. He has a Jewish landlord, rants about "minorities" and insinuates that Jews gave the atomic secrets to the Russians. He even kills his best friend who is Jewish. We see Hitler's shadow in the background, and Serling warns that people shouldn't take the bait of hatred and prejudice. Scott says to Ellen in "Black Leather Jackets" that Earth is a planet with hate.

This is also the theme of "Deaths-Head Revisited," about a former Nazi who goes back to Dachau for "nostalgia" and ghosts of the prisoners hold a trial for him for "crimes against humanity." The Nazi calls the prisoners "pigs" and laughs when he is sentenced to be insane. For Serling, insanity suits bigots, fascists and Nazis.

In "The Big Tall Wish" Bolie Jackson, an African-American boxer, tells his friend Henry, a little boy who plays with rabbits and believes in magic, that magic and dreams don't exist. Perhaps, like the poet Langston Hughes, Bolie believes that dreams do not exist for blacks in American society—this show was aired in 1960 with a black cast in a segregated society.[30] Serling had "long been a champion of equality" and according to him "it matters little, when a human being cries out, the color or creed of that human being."[31] The boy's mother struggles to make ends meet in a society where everyone isn't equal.

In "A Quality of Mercy" Serling makes a controversial move and mixes prejudice with war, putting an American soldier in the shoes of a Japanese soldier. The fact that these soldiers are of different races adds to the drama, as does the fact that the story is about two of the things that Serling is against: war and prejudice.

The story in "A Quality of Mercy" is set in the Philippine Islands, August 1945 with a group of American soldiers fighting Japanese soldiers who are in a cave. The American lieutenant wants to "pulverize" the enemy but when he refers to "the Japs" the American sergeant says "they're men, lieutenant." The sergeant asks the lieutenant when he'll be satisfied, the lieutenant says when they've killed all the enemy—"if they're the enemy, they get it. First day of the war or last day of the war—they get it."

The twist comes when the lieutenant's binoculars fall and he becomes Japanese. Now he's afraid. Now Americans are shooting at him. Now the Americans are in the cave and he has to decide whether to shoot them. Now there is a Japanese general who wants to go into the cave. Now he is not so sure he wants to kill the wounded Americans. The Japanese general says they must destroy the enemies. Now the lieutenant says "but they are men." The Japanese general compares the American soldiers to ants and uses the same dialogue that the American lieutenant had used: all of the Americans must be killed, first day or last day of the war.

The lieutenant is now an American. The American soldiers want to go into the cave for the Japanese soldiers but now he doesn't want to kill people and hopes that there will not be any more wars.

In "The Encounter" there is a current of prejudice—the American man and the Japanese gardener are still fighting WWII even after it's over as the gardener tries to get revenge.

"No Time Like the Past" has one of the tenants at the time traveler's, Paul Driscoll's, boarding house spouting some of the most appallingly racist comments of any of the shows. While Paul is offended by him he listens as the boarder speaks of American imperialism and how we should put the American flag in the "Orient" how giving land to the native Americans is "conciliatory nonsense" because "savages" cannot understand treaties and that we should destroy the "red skins." When Paul objects the boarder calls him a "pacifist" but Paul gives a speech to him about "armchair warriors" that Serling wrote and that we imagine Serling would have given had he been at that table.

Serling makes the point that prejudice is not only about racial or ethnic prejudice, although he discusses that in many of the shows, but it's also about prejudice against aliens ("The Gift") and our neighbors ("The Monsters are Due on Maple St."and "The Shelter"). In "Monsters" Serling reminds us that "there are weapons that are simply thoughts, attitudes, prejudices to be found only in the minds of men. Prejudices can kill and suspicion can destroy" and that these are not only in *The Twilight Zone.*

"I Am the Night Color Me Black" has one of the most eloquent speeches against hatred and prejudice by a black preacher. This story is about an execution—of a white man who murdered a "cross burning" bigot. But even though the prisoner may be innocent, and even though he murdered a bigot who whipped a black man, he enjoyed murdering him and so, according to the preacher, he's guilty. But the people who want to see him hang are also guilty—they haven't seen the light. The preacher says they are also guilty of hate and that's why the sky is black—after the man is executed other towns are black. Here is one of the only shows (the other is "Deaths-Head Revisited") where Serling does not say "in the Twilight Zone"—he says that hate is contagious and you look for it in the mirror, not the Twilight Zone.

Nuclear War

There are so many shows that feature the theme of nuclear war that we can say it is a ubiquitous theme of *The Twilight Zone*. Perhaps the most famous of those shows is "Time Enough at Last," where Mr. Bemis, played by Burgess Meredith, is the librarian who reads books in the bank vault when there is a nuclear bomb. But there are other shows, such as "Third from the Sun" and "The Shelter" about nuclear war.

According to Sander, Serling joined the Hollywood chapter of Citizens for a Sane Nuclear Policy, an anti-nuclear group, in 1955, the first American program to show the bomb exploding was "Time Enough at Last."[32]

The story of "One More Pallbearer" is about revenge but set in the worst scene that Serling could think of which was nuclear war. The scene is outside the Radin Building, named for and owned by Paul Radin a wealthy man who is inside wiring the basement to sound like a hydrogen bomb is going off. A movie plays with a hydrogen bomb going off and Mr. Radin says to the man wiring up the basement that it's not an illusion, just a good bomb shelter.

He invites three people into the shelter—note that this show is the flip side of "The Shelter" where people try to get into their neighbor's shelter but he won't let them in—a schoolteacher, a colonel and a preacher. The teacher failed Radin for cheating, the colonel court-martialed him, and the preacher accused him of a "lack of character." Paul has called them, and his chauffeur has forced them, there to settle "old scores." He wants to get back at them by putting them in the shelter and telling them about nuclear war. He tells them the shelter is composed of concrete, steel and lead—with a storehouse of food—and says that he knows that the bomb is going to explode over them that evening—the nuclear bomb, "they bomb us, we bomb them"—and there'll be nothing left but rubble.

They are safe in the shelter, and he asks them if they want to stay there and avoid the war. He plays a speaker of a civil defense warning about "an attack by enemy forces" and the warning says "if you are in your home go to your shelter." But it's fake, just like the nuclear war. A mobile in the background symbolizes the spinning atom. They hear air raid sirens—but rather than wanting to stay, they want to leave. Unlike "The Shelter," Radin says they can stay, he won't kick them out, but they must ask his forgiveness. The schoolteacher would rather spend the time alone or "with a stray cat." They want out.

He lets them out, but says they'll be back. They run out—they can't stay in the shelter—and the schoolteacher tells him that if he puts mirrors up he'll have "a world full of Radins" just like in "The Mind and the Matter" Beechcroft can have a world full of Beechcrofts. They leave, and he starts to believe the civil defense warning. He watches the film of the bomb and mushroom cloud. He emerges from the shelter and sees the rubble and no people—but it's only his illusion, as he tried to make his prisoners believe. He believes his own illusion as the people on the street walk by. He is driven crazy by his own illusion. He looks like he has been to war, as he looks at the rubble of his nuclear war—but it's only his, and nobody else's. Serling tries to think of the scariest thing he can—and that's nuclear war, the hydrogen bomb, the rubble and the shelter.

"The Shelter" is also a story that seems to be about nuclear war but isn't—like "The Monsters are Due on Maple St." it's about prejudice and its "fallout." The story of the neighbors at a party revolves around the theme of the shelter, but here it's for aliens. The aliens are landing on Earth and people are told to go to shelters. The theme here is that even though the neighbors think they are at war with aliens they are really at war with each other—the Hobbesian war of "all against all." They are not at war with aliens at all, but with each other, as Hobbes says. Serling uses the scene of nuclear war because that was a big theme when "The Shelter" was shown in 1961.

"Time Enough at Last," perhaps the most famous of *The Twilight Zone* shows with the theme of nuclear war, combines the themes of alienation and nuclear war, with Henry Bemis as the bank teller who is the only person after a nuclear war. Serling used bank buildings ("Person or Persons Unknown") and offices ("The Mind and the Matter," "Mr. Bevis") to show alienation of modern society. Here, Serling wonders which he prefers—working as a bank teller, which bores Mr. Bemis, or being the only person after nuclear war with a library of books to read. Serling prefers the latter until the broken glasses.

Serling's message is that nuclear war and alienation are both creations of modernity—and two of the themes he hates about modernity. Serling also shows an alienated marriage, with Mr. Bemis' wife ripping up his poetry books (like in "Escape Clause" where Walter calls his wife a "potato pancake"). For Serling, alienation and nuclear war are two themes here, in perhaps the greatest show of *The Twilight Zone*, suggesting people invent bombs and nuclear war because they are alienated. Modern society includes alienated marriages, alienated societies and alienated countries that go to nuclear war.

In "On Thursday We Leave for Home" the Colonel who rescues the people says "through a miracle . . . we never had the hydrogen war" but in "Elegy," written by Charles Beaumont, the astronaut says the nuclear war was in 1985. The nuclear rubble after the bomb seems like an ideal place for Mr. Bemis to read, at the library—but when his glasses break he is back to his alienation. In "Probe 7 Over and Out" Colonel Cook crash lands on a planet—a nuclear war is about to start on the planet he left. Countries are bombing each other and the only safe place is outer space. Cook meets Norda—who calls herself Eve—and they call the planet Earth. The idea here is that people on Earth and the Garden of Eden came here to escape nuclear war on their planet.

This is the same theme in "Third from the Sun" written by Serling based on a short story by Richard Matheson, and aired at the height of the cold war in January 1960, scientists at a "hydrogen armaments" plant discuss nuclear war that they believe will happen—their country will drop a bomb on the enemy and the enemy will retaliate.

A scientist at the plant, William Sturka, decides he is going to leave. His daughter asks him how he can like a job where he makes hydrogen bombs and he says there are lots of people who work on each part of a bomb, thereby trying to take responsibility away from himself.

This is a family on the eve of nuclear war. The daughter, Jody, says that everyone is afraid. Sturka says that people are afraid because they scare themselves by subverting great ideas—i.e., people subverted Einstein's ideas to make bombs. There is a starburst clock over the fireplace symbolizing the sun of the planet Earth. His wife, Eve, says that she is afraid and he tells her that nuclear war, a "holocaust" is coming in 48 hours and they're leaving. A statue of a girl is in their room symbolic of Jody—Sturka's daughter and also Rod Serling's daughter.[33] We could also think of the poet Lathbury's poem here, the poem from "No Time Like the Past," but here it's: "children of today, heirs of tomorrow, what are *we* weaving, labor and sorrow?" Serling makes the point, with the statue of the child, that a planet's future depends on children and preventing nuclear war.

While Sturka is planning his escape the plant manager is spying on them. Sturka invites his friends, Jerry and Ann, over for lemonade. They are going to a planet 11 million miles away—but they're willing to go because, as Sturka says, it's better than staying. Jerry says that with a couple of breaks they could get there. Carling, the plant manager, comes to Sturka's house. He goes outside and wonders if there are people on other planets and if Sturka would be happier there.

Meanwhile, Sturka plans the escape and says the planet will blow itself up, but they'll be out in space. The phone rings. It's an Erica phone, popular and "space age" at the time. It's the plant. They want Sturka to work. Sturka and Jerry drive there to escape on a spaceship. It's a flying saucer. But Carling is there with a gun. He doesn't want them to escape. Jody pushes the gun out of his hand—it's the younger generation that will stop nuclear war, just as Jody pushes away the gun of the manager of the hydrogen bomb plant.

The next scene is on the spaceship, the Sturkas and Jerry and Ann escaped. Where are they going? To the "third planet form the sun" a place called Earth. They're escaping from nuclear war on a different planet. The idea is that people, on any planet, always try to blow themselves up—but if we blow up Earth where can we escape to?

"Two," by Montgomery Pittman, is an interesting portrayal of two people left in the rubble of nuclear war. This show opens season three of *The Twilight Zone*, which also includes "The Shelter," "It's A Good Life," "To Serve Man." There is no dialogue, the opening scene is a bombed out city where there are no people.

A woman walks through the town and a man approaches. They fight over canned food—what people stocked their bomb shelters with in the 1950s— and scarce resources. The man says the war is over so they shouldn't fight, Serling's hope that after WWII there wouldn't be a World War. Because there are no more governments there is no reason to fight—the idea that belligerence is not part of human nature but part of government and people are warlike because of society.

The man says he wants peace. These two, he speaks English and she is Russian (she says "prokrazny") walk off together into the sunset, but with guns.

"The Old Man in the Cave," based on a short story "The Old Man," by Henry Slesar, is a story about a town after nuclear war. The scene is 1974, ten years after nuclear war. A horse drawn car opens the scene (Serling likes to use a horse drawn carriage to symbolize the nineteenth century) and there are only 500 people left between Buffalo and Georgia.

A militia soldier, Major French, comes to town in a jeep and the leader of the people, Goldsmith, tells him that the Old Man in the Cave is their leader. French wants to know why they do not eat the canned food—they look thin. Goldsmith says that the old man in the cave tells them where to plant, what to eat, how to stay away from fallout, etc. and told them not to eat the canned food. This is one of the shows where people are in the "state of nature" with no government. In the state of nature a bully, like French, can be the leader. He wants to see the old man in the cave—it's a computer and the people stone it. Major French says "you're free." The next scene shows the people lying on the ground. Goldsmith is the only one who listened to the computer and didn't eat the canned food.

People after nuclear war have no elected leaders so they choose a leader, a computer, which was wiser than humans because it does not have their war-like human nature. Goldsmith says the old man in the cave didn't drop the bomb, he didn't blow up the Earth. Serling realizes that if the world were run by computers that don't have the belligerent nature there would be no belligerence and therefore no wars (although, in "From Agnes with Love," written by Bernard C. Shoenfeld, the computer has emotions). Here, the computer actually helps them.

Alienation

For Marx, the thing about the twentieth century was alienation, and for Marc Scott Zicree the thing about *The Twilight Zone* was alienation.[34] Alexis de Tocqueville, in *Democracy in America*, said the "isolation of men from one another" and their "selfishness"[35] was the theme of America. In his Introduction to "Alienation," Bertell Ollman says that Marx's "theory of alienation places the acting and acted upon individual in the center of this account. In this theory, man himself is offered as the vantage point from which to view his own relations."[36] This is very much in keeping with the themes of *The Twilight Zone*—the individual, human nature, and individual alienation in modern society.

As in "The Brain Center at Whipple's," Marx says:

> the worker becomes all the poorer the more wealth he produces, the more his production increases in power and range. The worker becomes an ever cheaper commodity the more commodities he creates. With the *increasing value* of the world of things proceeds in direct proportion the *devaluation* of the world of men. Labor produces not only commodities: it produces itself and the worker as a commodity. . . .[37]

This theme is also in "Steel" where a boxer becomes a commodity, and we can see other shows where people are commodities—such as "Stopover in a Quiet Town," where a couple becomes toys for an alien child and "People are Alike All Over" where an Earthling is put in a zoo from another planet. Alienation can also be considered a theme in: "From Agnes with Love," "What's In the Box?," "The Fear," "The Monsters are Due on Maple St.," "Miniature," "Mr. Bevis," "The Obsolete Man," "Person or Persons Unknown," "The Changing of the Guard," "People are Alike All Over," "The Lonely," "A Stop at Willoughby," and "Where Is Everybody?"

"The Masks" is about a family alienated by money, "From Agnes with Love" is about a scientist alienated from his work by a computer that falls in love with him and drives him crazy, "What's in the Box?" is a story of domestic violence and an alienated couple as is "The Bewitchin' Pool." People are alienated by technology in: "The Brain Center at Whipple's," "Living Doll," "From Agnes with Love," "The Lonely," "A Thing About Machines," "The Lateness of the Hour," "The Long Morrow," and others and turn into robots in "The Brain Center at Whipple's," "Uncle Simon," "The Lateness of the Hour," "In His Image," "I Sing the Body Electric," and "Steel," where boxing is done by robots. In "The After Hours" mannequins turn into people and then back into mannequins symbolizing the alienation of humans into commodities, mannequins, for the company.[38] To the capitalists, workers are commodities, mannequins, and when the mannequins want to turn into people that means they want freedom from their servitude. Turning into a robot is the height of alienation. The fact that Serling uses mannequins and robots interchangeably with people symbolizes the alienation of people from themselves and each other in modern society where you are alienated from yourself so much that you are automated—not even human.

In "Stopover In a Quiet Town," written by Earl Hamner, Jr., a couple wakes up in a strange bed not knowing where they are. This is alienation, and sounds like Marx who calls capitalism ". . . a dwelling which he cannot look upon as his own home where he might at last exclaim, 'Here I am at home,' but where instead he finds himself in someone else's house, in the house of a stranger who daily lies in wait for him. . . ."[39] Everything is a commodity—the food in the refrigerator is fake, the squirrel is fake, even the grass is fake. A man in a car is a dummy. They say "something came down on the car from overhead" while they were driving—aliens took them to their planet where they are used for toys. This is alienation and also alien-ation with aliens! The couple is a commodity—toys for a space alien child. Just as these people don't belong to themselves, but to the space alien who has appropriated them, people in capitalist society don't belong to themselves because they and their work are appropriated by capitalists.

For the astronaut Sam Conrad in "People Are Alike All Over" this is not only alienation, but alien-ation when he is put in a zoo with the title "Earth creature in his native habitat." Sam Conrad is alienated because he is used as a commodity and, as Marx said "finds himself in someone else's house" and even on someone else's planet. He is an alien, and perhaps this is why Serling liked the use of aliens—because they symbolized "alien-ation" that people were being alienated from themselves just as Earthlings were alienated from aliens as in "To Serve Man" and others. Marx says "he is also aware of the contrast in quality between his dwelling and a human dwelling—a residence in that *other* world. . . ."[40] Also "Estrangement is manifested . . . in the fact that . . . all is under the sway of inhuman power."[41] Perhaps for Serling the alien is a symbol of how people are used, alienated, and made into commodities in modern society.

"Person or Persons Unknown," written by Charles Beaumont, symbolizes modern alienation of people from other people—family, people at work— and man from himself, which is also a theme in "The Mind and the Matter," "A World of Difference," and "Mr. Bevis."

A man, David Gurney, wakes up and his wife doesn't know who he is. He is a stranger—she's never seen him. He doesn't have an identity and this symbolizes the alienation of man in modern capitalist society. He doesn't even know who he is because he doesn't have his license, or an ID issued by the state, which tells you who you are.

After his alienation at home he goes to his office at the bank, where he is also alienated from his fellow workers. They don't know him. He goes to a psychiatrist—alienated people are crazy—where a man thinks he's Winston Churchill but nobody knows who he is either. David's best friend doesn't know him, his mother doesn't know him. He is not listed in the phonebook. He asks "who am I?"

He jumps out of a window and runs from the police to the bar where he hangs out. The bartender doesn't know him. He thinks there's a conspiracy against him. He realizes that he took a picture with his wife—he goes to the photo store to get it but when the psychiatrist looks at the picture he is the only one in the picture. He falls down and pounds the floor. But it was just a dream and he wakes up. Now his wife is the one who *he* doesn't know—now no one knows who *she* is. Now she is alienated.

This is modernity, the impersonal, and alienating world of bank clerks and strangers of *The Twilight Zone*.

"A World of Difference," written by Richard Matheson, has the theme of alienation from a man's work, family and self. According to Marc Zicree, "the issues of alienation and the nature of reality would dominate the sixties and the years beyond."[42] In "A World of Difference" a man playing a character in a television show believes he is the character. Again, as in "Person or Persons," he doesn't know his identity. He does not know real from pretend and cannot separate his work world from his home world—as Marx says "what is animal becomes human and what is human becomes animal."[43]

Arthur Curtis is a character in a movie played by Jerry Raigan. Serling calls this "a tableau of reality"—Jerry Raigan thinks he's Curtis. He looks at the crew and wonders what they're doing in his house. He doesn't know where he is. He doesn't know his wife—he knows Curtis' wife. He tries to go to Curtis' house in Woodland Hills, but when he gets there it's not familiar. Jerry says he wants to go home, but he doesn't know where that is—even at his house. He tries to look up Curtis in the phone book and call the company he works for. They show Jerry the movie script and the cast of characters, including the character played by him but he still thinks he's not who he is. His confusion demonstrates the thin identity of those in alienated modern society.

"A World of Difference" is about escape from the alienation of modern society, just like Willoughby is about escape in "A Stop at Willoughby." Jerry Raigan escapes, as his co-worker admits he'd like to—to a "simpler" place away from the "turmoil." When they stop work on the movie there is no character. Jerry escapes with his movie wife into a fantasy and they go on vacation—he escapes into another script.

Just as a computer falls in love with a man in "From Agnes with Love," and a man falls in love with a computer in "The Lonely," in "Miniature" a man falls in love with a doll. "Miniature," written by Charles Beaumont, is about a man so alienated from people that the only "person" he can relate to is a doll in a museum miniature scene. The scene opens with Charley Parkes in the cubicle of his office. There are other office workers there, in an office pool. This symbol of alienation, the office pool and cubicle, is also shown in "The Mind and the Matter" and "Mr. Bevis," to symbolize conformity and alienation.

Charley Parkes goes to the museum for lunch and wanders away from the crowd of tourists to the dollhouses. He picks out one with a doll playing a piano in a Victorian parlor, as Serling says he goes to the museum to be alone. Charley thinks he hears music, the doll is playing the piano. But the doll is a block of wood and the security guard thinks Charley is hallucinating.

Because Charley was at the museum talking to the doll his boss fires him. His boss alienates him by calling him a "wind up toy" with no humanity, asks him if he likes the workers, and says the office is a team and it doesn't work because Charley doesn't fit in.

Charley goes home and tells his mother that his boss fired him. His mother asks why he always makes people uncomfortable. Meanwhile, back at the museum there is a soap opera at the dollhouse where the doll dates an abusive boyfriend. Charley's sister follows him to the museum and sees him at the dollhouse. She introduces him to a lady and they go on a date but he throws her off the park bench. He tells the doll about the date.

When the doll's boyfriend assaults her Charley breaks the glass to the dollhouse. He is taken to a psychiatrist where he stays for a few days. He is having a psychotic break, alienation makes people psychotic, and the psychiatrist gives him the doll—it's wood. The psychiatrist says the pressure of trying to conform contributed to the breakdown.

Charley is unable to cope with the modern world. They were going to use shock treatment to further alienate him, his brother-in-law comments that there must be a lot of "nuts" there, but they let him go home. They make another date with the lady that his sister introduced him to and Charley goes out the window—just as in "Person or Persons Unknown"—he flees his house to be with the doll. His family chases him, with the psychiatrist and police, to the museum and he hides among the Egyptian art. As the police and the psychiatrist arrive at the museum the security guard looks in the dollhouse and Charley is sitting in the dollhouse with the doll.

Charley's alienation from the world makes him want to be with a doll—just as alienation makes Corry want to be with a robot Alicia in "The Lonely." They say that Charley needed a "simple world" but as he says: any world with people is not simple—there's always "loneliness" and he says he's been lonely all his life.

Alienation is the theme of "Where is Everybody?" which is the first show of season 1 of *The Twilight Zone*. So *The Twilight Zone* starts with the theme of alienation—with an experiment to see how astronauts behave when they are alone on other planets. Here, a man walks in the mist and through an empty café, an empty town. He is alone. We see people from the Air Force and a closed circuit TV conducting an experiment to see how he would react to being alone. Serling's voiceover reminds us about man's "hunger for companionship, the barrier of loneliness."

The "hunger for companionship" is also a theme of "The Lonely," where Corry is a prisoner on a planet and lives in isolation. He feels "like an animal in a cage" but when the people from Earth bring him a robot woman he isn't lonely anymore. When they don't have room in the spaceship to take the robot Alicia back to Earth he says he doesn't want to leave without her—but the captain says "all you're leaving behind is loneliness."

"The After Hours" is a story about mannequins who become people and then go back to being mannequins, or commodities, in a store. Marsha White is shopping for a gold thimble in a store and she takes the express elevator to the ninth floor—but there is no ninth floor. She is on an empty floor—it's a shell of a store just as she is a shell, a mannequin who wants to be a person. A saleslady shows her the one item in an empty showroom—the thimble—and knows her name. Marsha buys the thimble and takes the elevator back down but then sees the thimble is scratched and goes to complaints where they tell her there is no ninth floor.

Marsha sees the saleslady who sold her the thimble is a mannequin. The mannequin talks to her and all the mannequins in the store talk to her. She realizes she is a mannequin and she was a person for a month—but now she goes back to being a mannequin. When a mannequin asks Marsha if it was fun being a person she says yes. The background music is *The Emperor Waltz*, as if to show that people are royalty but mannequins are just commodities. Serling asks: "just who are the people we say our hellos to?"

Loneliness, isolation and alienation from the world and particularly modern society are the themes of other *Twilight Zone* shows, perhaps because Serling felt alienated from the modern world of nameless and faceless crowds in cities, workers like cogs in wheels, and alienation of people from community. Because community was so important to Serling, he did not like the isolation of individualism and anonymity of modern society.

As de Tocqueville said traditional society had "made a chain of all the members of the community . . . democracy breaks that chain."[44] So that for de Tocqueville, and Serling, society in America was individuals but not held as a community with interests, just alienated people, "Each of them, living apart, is as a stranger to the fate of all the rest . . . as for his fellow citizens, he is close to them, but does not see them; he touches them, but he does not feel them; he exists only in himself and for himself alone. . . ."[45] The alienated people could turn to a fascist dictator because they were alienated from each other and, according to De Tocqueville, "these two things perniciously complete and assist each other. Equality places men side by side, unconnected by any common tie . . ." fascism "raises barriers to keep them" apart.

De Tocqueville was talking about nineteenth century America, which Serling wrote about in shows like "A Stop at Willoughby" and "No Time like the Past." De Tocqueville imagined that America would become more alienated, more equal and less free, a place where Henry David Thoreau would go to Walden Pond to escape and the alienation trend would give government more rights but people less freedom. This was De Tocqueville's discussion about alienation during the time in America that Serling harks back to with nostalgia.

Serling used Buster Keaton in a show about the nineteenth versus the twentieth century called "Once Upon a Time," written by Richard Matheson. Here, Woodrow Mulligan, a janitor in Harmony, New York, in 1890, thinks that everything is too expensive and there is too much noise. He sees steak for 17 cents a pound and he hears a blacksmith hitting an anvil to the theme of "The Anvil Chorus." A horse and carriage, Serling's symbol of the nineteenth century, drive by. Mulligan is a critic of the nineteenth century so when he goes to the basement of his employer, Professor Gilbert, the clothesline and washtub and wringer are also symbols of the nineteenth century.

Professor Gilbert invents a Time Helmet, if you wear it you can go to any year for 30 minutes. Woodrow wants to escape the nineteenth century and go where there's "peace and quiet." He puts on the helmet and goes to 1962. Now, sirloin steak is $1.19 a pound. He's in Harmony, but he hears noise—traffic, road noise, etc. (when Woodrow gets to the twentieth century we hear sound). He decides that he wants to go back to 1890, but he has 15 minutes to get back and the helmet is damaged. He sees a TV, a typewriter, and a vacuum cleaner—all modern "conveniences" which, according to Woodrow and Rousseau, are not conveniences because they break.

Woodrow walks around in his underwear because he left his pants in 1890. He steals a pair of pants, which his friend pays for, and the helmet is fixed. His friend, a scientist he met, says that 1890 is great and calls the nineteenth century "the halcyon days" that are "charming." Woodrow pays the man who fixed the helmet with money from the pants he stole. The scientist puts the helmet on to go back to the "halcyon days" and Woodrow holds on to him and they both go back to 1890.

The scientist says "charming, charming" of the nineteenth century and Woodrow is happy he is back in the nineteenth century—he sees the prices are cheap. But when the scientist sees there are no modern "conveniences" like TV dinners he wants to go back to the twentieth century. Woodrow puts the hat on him and we assume he goes back—although we don't know if he does because we don't see him. Also, he's been in 1890 for a week so how does he get back? Perhaps the man made some "minor adjustments" and fixed the hat so that the scientist could stay for more than 30 minutes. This is unexplained, as is the money that comes from the pants Woodrow stole—but the message is clear: maybe we glamorize the past too much, but then again, maybe we like our conveniences too much.

Notes

1. Hobbes, *Leviathan*, Introduction.
2. This is similar to the themes of "Uncle Simon" and "The Masks" which are also set in mansions.
3. This was written by Ray Bradbury and is a reference to Walt Whitman's "I sing the body electric" "all is procession; the universe is a procession, with measured and beautiful motion." When Whitman speaks of the body "electric" clearly he is speaking too of the industrial revolution and machine power and modernity.
4. Jack Warden, from "The Lonely" plays the team's manager.
5. Playing a similar part to Dr. Loren in "The Lateness of the Hour."
6. A group in the nineteenth century who smashed machines because they thought they would take their jobs.
7. John Pietaro says this is the strongest statement in *The Twilight Zone* on behalf of the working class, Rod Serling, For Your Consideration in P*olitical Affairs* Magazine http://www.politicalaffairs.net/article/articleview/7940/.
8. Marx, "Communist Manifesto."
9. Marx, "Communist Manifesto."
10. Sander, Gordon F., *Serling: The Rise and Twilight of Television's Last Angry Man* (Dutton: NY, 1992) p. 155.
11. Sander, p. 12.
12. Sander, p. 13.
13. Sander, p. 21. Sander says the "Seurat-like gazebo" featured in "A Stop at Willoughby" is still in Binghamtom, p. 11. The Rod Serling Foundation put a plaque in the gazebo in Recreation Park, Binghamton, as the idea for Serling's "Walking Distance." The park also features a carousel and bandstand concerts according to its website, www.westsidebinghamton.org/recpark.html, where you can see the gazebo and Rod Serling Memorial plaque for the gazebo which says "Rod Serling, Creator of the Twilight Zone, 'Walking Distance.'"
14. "Submitted for Your Approval," *American Masters*, PBS TV show produced and directed by Susan Lacy and written by Thomas Wagner and John Goff, 1995.

15. Jodi Serling, in "Submitted for your approval," *American Masters*, PBS TV show.

16. Epictetus, *The Art of Living: The Classic Manual on Virtue, Happiness, and Effectiveness*, A New Interpretation by Sharon Lebell (Harper Collins: NY, 1995) p. 22.

17. Sander, p. 129.

18. "Submitted for Your Approval," *American Masters*, PBS television show, produced, and directed by Susan Lacy and written by Thomas Wagner and John Goff, 1995.

19. Sander, p.3–4. *The Velvet Alley* was a show about a Hollywood writer, written by Serling for TV in 1959.

20. Quoted in CBS VHS video, Oct. 1959, *Treasures of The Twilight Zone*.

21. Quoted in CBS VHS video, Oct. 1959, *Treasures of The Twilight Zone*.

22. Liner notes to *The Twilight Zone* VHS, by Marc Scott Zicree, author of *The Twilight Zone Companion*, Columbia House video.

23. Liner notes to *The Twilight Zone* VHS, by Marc Scott Zicree, author of *The Twilight Zone Companion*, Columbia House video. In "The Fugitive" (1962) Jenny asks Ben, "Are you a criminal? What'd you do? Rob a bank, kill somebody?" He says no. "Then you must be a Communist." Thanks to Clifford Feldman for this reference.

24. His friends had been affected by anti-communist hearings according to *American Masters*, "Submitted for your approval," PBS TV show.

25. Apparently the feeling was mutual. In 1963 the Kennedy administration recruited Serling to do seminars and act as a "goodwill" ambassador to Australia and the South Pacific, Sander, p. 189. In 1964 the U.S. Information Agency asked him to make a documentary about the Kennedy assassination called *Let Us Continue*. Rod Serling Resource site, www.danville.lib.il.us/Pathfinder/rodvid.html. The term "Cold War" comes from the essay "You and the Atomic Bomb" by George Orwell, October 1945.

26. Tom Paine, *Common Sense*, (Penguin: NY 1986) edited with an Intro by Isaac Kramnick, p. 98.

27. *TV Guide* interview, April 21, 1962.

28. Serling, *LA Times*, June 25, 1967 interview "Serling in Creative Mainstream" by Ellen Cameron May.

29. "Submitted for Your Approval," *American Masters*, PBS, 1995.

30. See *A Dream Deferred* by Langston Hughes, also John Pietaro discusses this aspect of racism in *Rod Serling, For Your Consideration* in http://www.politicalaffairs.net/article/articleview/7940/.

31. Liner notes, Columbia House video "The Big Tall Wish."

32. Sander, Gordon, p. 155 *Serling: The Rise and Twilight of Television's Last Angry Man* (Dutton: NY, 1992). He also used the theme of nuclear war in a television movie "Carol for another Christmas" aired once on December 28, 1964.

33. According to Zicree this story about nuclear war was so important for Serling that he named the character Jody for his daughter, liner notes to CBS video.

34. Zicree, Marc Scott, Author's Note on the Second edition to *Twilight Zone Companion* (Silman-James Press, Los Angeles 1989).

35. Alexis de Tocqueville, *Democracy in America*, "Individualism stronger at the close of a democratic revolution" Modern Library, NY 1945 with an introduction by Thomas Bender, p. 398.

36. Ollman, Bertell, *Alienation: Marx's Conception of Man in Capitalist Society* 2nd edition (Cambridge University Press: NY, 1976) p. xi.

37. Marx, Karl, "Economic and Philosophic Manuscripts of 1844" in *Marx and Engels Reader,* edited by Robert C. Tucker (W.W. Norton: NY, 1978) p.71.

38. Michael Moore uses this symbol in *Roger and Me,* where he shows people at a party hired to be mannequins for the rich.

39. Marx, Karl, "Economic and Philosophic Manuscripts of 1844" quoted in *Marx and Engels Reader,* p. 100.

40. Ibid, p. 100 clearly Marx was not referring to aliens, but to money and profit which he considered "alien."

41. *Ibid.,* Marx, p. 100.

42. Zicree, liner notes to CBS video *A World of Difference.*

43. Marx, "Economic and Philosophic Manuscripts of 1844," p. 74.

44. Alexis de Tocqueville, *Democracy in America,* "Individualism in Democratic Countries" Modern Library, NY 1945, abridged with an introduction by Thomas Bender, p. 397.

45. Alexis de Tocqueville, Democracy in America, Modern Library, p. 583.

4

Magic and Optimism

We are all in the gutter, but some of us are looking at the stars.

—Oscar Wilde, *Lady Windermere's Fan*, Act III, 1892

Magic

Although many of *The Twilight Zone*'s themes are pessimistic with negative or twist endings that illustrate man's inhumanity to man, and the nastiness and negative aspects of human nature, others express the power of human goodness and magic. Marc Scott Zicree said that the thing about Serling and *The Twilight Zone* was the theme of alienation—man's alienation from his work, himself and his fellow man.[1] But in spite of this we can see many optimistic elements, including children and their association with magic—featured in "The Big Tall Wish," "The Gift," "Long Distance Call"—and magic in many shows including "The Night of the Meek" and others which allude to Serling's abiding confidence in the mind and the spirit of people and human nature, even considering the character from "The Mind and the Matter" and his claim that "people are pigs."

Magic is so powerful in many of these episodes that we cannot dismiss it. It is particularly powerful in "The Big Tall Wish," where Serling employs the themes of boxing and children to create the magic. Bolie Jackson is a down and out boxer who is looking for a comeback and Serling says he might want to look for some magic as he looks into a mirror and we see Henry, a boy who is his friend, reflected in the mirror. Henry makes what he calls big, tall wishes for things that he wants—and he gets them. He made a big, tall wish for his mother and someone sent her $15 so she could pay her rent.

Bolie Jackson wonders when kids stop believing in magic. For him, there is no magic, just a concrete world. Bolie is a realist with a negative view of the world but for Serling he is someone who refuses to believe in mysteries or magic. Bolie goes into the comeback fight with the attitude that there is no magic, but because he doesn't believe in magic he loses the fight. The fight is televised and on the other side of the TV Henry is wishing for Bolie—and Bolie wins! Henry's big, tall wish made him win. Henry tells Bolie they needed magic and that's when he made the big, tall wish. But Bolie must believe, only then will the magic work—only if you believe. Bolie tells Henry he's too old to believe—he is defeated.

Not only is Bolie defeated, but he talks Henry out of believing in magic. Henry now says there is no magic and Bolie says there just aren't enough people to believe. Serling's voiceover says it's strange that people refuse to embrace miracles. Bolie realizes that his failure to believe made him lose and if we don't have the ability to believe then dreams won't come true. In a scene that reinforces Henry's belief in magic, we see him go to the roof of his building to tend rabbits, the tool of the magician—but he won't be pulling any out of hats because only kids believe in magic, so he doesn't.

Some might see "The Big Tall Wish" as a statement that with maturity there is no magic. Bolie not only doesn't believe in magic, but talks Henry out of it. Rather than being a negative message, it can be optimistic—the idea that all you need is to believe in magic. Serling plays against the idea that with maturity there is no magic in "Kick the Can," "Static," "Night of the Meek," "Changing of the Guard," and "The Trade-Ins."

Serling also uses the theme of children and magic in "The Gift" and "Long Distance Call" by William Idelson and Charles Beaumont. "The Gift" is a story about a boy, Pedro, who takes care of an alien who crashes his spaceship in his Mexican town. Pedro is called a "stargazer" and he is the only person who is not afraid of the alien. Pedro says "I am an odd one" and is compared to an "old man" because he is wise. "Long Distance Call" also uses the theme with a boy, Billy, who uses a magic phone to call the other side.

The idea that you need to believe in magic in order for it to work, that miracles happen only if people believe, is also the theme of "Dust." According to Serling, this hot and dusty Western town is a place where people fight against themselves. A Mexican man, Luis Gallegos, has accidently killed a child while driving his wagon while intoxicated. He is going to hang. Sykes is a sleazy peddler who taunts Gallegos from outside the jail. Sykes is a bigot who accuses the sheriff of sympathy for foreigners.

Luis' father believes in magic—he has a magic coin. Sykes takes advantage of this by selling him "magic dust" that turns hate to love for 100 pesos. Again, as in "The Big Tall Wish," a child, Luis' daughter, is employed. But the "magic" dust is just dirt that Sykes picks up from the ground and puts in a bag. Echoing the idea that "people are pigs" the sheriff says that when the Earth was made the Creator should have stopped before making people.

But if you believe, the magic works and as Luis is at the gallows his father buys the "magic" dust and sprinkles it on the crowd as they laugh at him. It turns hate to love according to Sykes, the peddler, who is amazed when it actually works. And it works because Luis' father believes in magic and tells the crowd to pay heed to the magic

When they hang Luis the rope breaks—the magic works even though it was a five-strand rope. Sheriff Koch asks the Canfields, whose daughter was killed in the accident, if they should try the hanging again—they say no. The magic triumphs. The Canfields believe the magic too and so does Sykes, for whom hate turns to love when he gives the Mexican children the gold coins, gold pesos for which he sold the dust. Sykes agrees that it's magic, it must be magic and Serling's voiceover reminds us that we have to look inside ourselves to make magic.

Magic also works for Mr. Denton in "Mr. Denton on Doomsday," as we see alcoholic cowboy Al Denton kick his dependency with the help of a peddler's magic potion. Al is the town drunk who was a gunslinger before he became an alcoholic. We see him standing outside of the bar in a wild west town where he is taunted by another cowboy, Dan. Al finds a gun in the street and Dan challenges him to a gunfight. Al shoots the gun out of Dan's hand. Al shoots the chandelier in the bar and it falls on Dan—with the town peddler looking on. Al turns down a drink offered to him by the bartender who also offers him words against guns.

Al is challenged to a gunfight by another cowboy and while he is practicing, and considering leaving town, he sees the peddler, Henry J. Fate, outside his window. Fate tells Al not to run away. Al curses the gun and Fate gives Al a potion—to become the fastest gun in town, but it only lasts for 10 seconds. Al drinks the potion and shoots out the streetlight—"The Night Fate Stepped In."

The next day Al meets Grant at the shootout in the bar. Al drinks the potion—but Grant also has the potion and they shoot each other at the same time. Both get shot in the hand and both will never be able to shoot again. This is good from Al's point of view and also Serling's who seems to use an anti-gun message here. Fate, or magic, saves Al from a life of drinking and of guns.

Perhaps the most optimistic show is "The Night of the Meek" which continues the theme of magic and the need for belief in it in order for it to work. Art Carney is a store Santa, Corwin, who throws back a few drinks at the bar before going to work. He stumbles and falls on the sidewalk. Rod Serling comes on and says Mr. Corwin is about to enter a world full of Christmas cheer and magic.

At work, Corwin falls off the Santa's chair because, as the bratty kid says, "he's loaded" as his mother, in a mink coat, shuffles him away. She is a pompous creep who doesn't know the true meaning of Christmas. But Corwin's boss, Mr. Dundee, fires him. Corwin drinks because he wants to believe that it's real—the North Pole and the elves. He wants to see the "dreamless" inherit the Earth.

As Corwin walks the street in his Santa suit he hears bells and, as the snow falls, he stumbles upon an alley and sees a sack of toys which he picks up. It's a magic sack and he stops at the homeless mission and gives out gifts—just what they want. When a policeman comes in Corwin says he's intoxicated with magic. He's hauled down to the police station for "stolen loot." But when Mr. Dundee comes down the bag only gives out garbage. Officer Flaherty calls the magic bag "supernatural" but just as Mr. Dundee is screaming about "abracadabra" the bag produces vintage cherry brandy for him. Corwin gives out the gifts to the kids—he doesn't want anything for himself just to make others happy.

Corwin goes back to the alley and sees a sled and reindeer—and an elf! All he had to do was believe. He sits on the sleigh next to the elf and they take off. Just then, Mr. Dundee and Officer Flaherty emerge from the station house inebriated and see Corwin in the sleigh riding high above them. The magic works—Dundee, formerly a Scrooge, puts his arm around Flaherty and invites him to come home with him for more holiday cheer and calls it a "remarkable" Christmas eve. Serling's voiceover addresses the people of the twentieth century to remind them there is magic to Christmas if people look to themselves.

Serling has an upbeat view of senior citizens, who are also associated with magic, and they are the subject of a variety of shows including "Kick the Can," "The Trade-Ins," "What You Need," "One for the Angels," "Static," and "Ninety Years without Slumbering" where they are usually outwitting, not outwitted. He also shows senior citizens as conniving and greedy, as in "Queen of the Nile" and "Uncle Simon" but there are many more shows in the spirit of the "Trade-Ins" and "The Changing of the Guard."

"The Changing of the Guard" has the similarly optimistic theme that people should look to themselves for magic. The show is set at the Rock Spring School for Boys in Rock Spring, Vermont where Professor Ellis Fowler reads to the students from "A Shropshire Lad" by A.E. Housman. He is a bespectacled pedant and it's the last day of the semester before Christmas vacation. He's taught for 51 years. He is called into the Headmaster's who tells him that his contract won't be renewed even though he is a teacher of "incalculable value." But there will be a changing of the guard.

Professor Fowler goes home and takes his gun out of a locked drawer as he listens to Handel's *Messiah*. He considers himself a failure—he's left nothing and accomplished nothing. He tells his housekeeper, Mrs. Landers, that he's not hungry and he's going to take a nap but instead he goes to the school with gun in hand. As he stands in front of the statue of Horace Mann, presumably the school's founder (and the founder of Antioch College) he reads Mann's words "Be ashamed to die until you have won some victory for humanity" and the class bells ring. He wonders why they are ringing at night. Out of habit he goes to his classroom (later one of the students recites "For Whom the Bell Tolls") and it's empty but soon it fills with ghosts of the boys he taught who helped win victories for mankind at Iwo Jima and Pearl Harbor.

As if by magic they come back, like in *A Christmas Carol*, and Fowler is speechless at their gratitude and the fact that he influenced them. The bells toll again and they disappear. Fowler goes home happy for dinner with Mrs. Landers. He listens to the carolers outside his window (like Scrooge) now with the idea that he helped others to win the victories for mankind.

The idea that all you need is to believe in magic, and also its association with children, is the optimistic theme of "Kick the Can" by George Clayton Johnson. The story is set at the Sunnyvale Rest Home for the aged. The place is antiquated and looks like one of those upstate, New York, mansions with the mansard roof.

One of the residents, Charles, says his son is coming to pick him up—but is left behind as the Sunnyvale residents watch kids playing kick the can in the street. Charles doesn't go back to the porch, but sits under a tree dreaming and watching the kids. His roommate, Ben, complains about the kids making noise but Charles doesn't mind the sounds of kick the can. He tells his roommate when they play games it keeps them young. This is a familiar ring of Plato in *The Republic* about the importance of games "But when children play the right games from the beginning and absorb lawfulness from music and poetry, it follows them in everything and fosters their growth, correcting anything in the city that may have gone wrong before—in other words, the very opposite of what happens where the games are lawless."[2]

Charles wonders why Ben does not believe in magic—when he was a kid he believed in the tooth fairy. What happened? Like Bolie Jackson, Ben says that he grew up. Fed up with the nonsense of maturity, Charles decides to run through a sprinkler with his clothes on and the director of the home thinks he needs to be segregated from the other residents.

Charles leads a rebellion by waiting until it's night and waking up the residents and telling them the secret of youth: games. He hears imaginary kids playing and implores them to play because believing that you are old makes you old. He then discourses on magic—there is magic in the world, he knows it—there is magic in love and friendship, and in games which are the greatest magic and particularly kick the can.

Charles leads the residents outside and when Ben and the director go outside they see kids playing. Ben sees Charles as a boy—a theme used in "Walking Distance" and also in "The Incredible World of Horace Ford" (by Reginald Rose)—and asks Charles to take him too but Charles and the other children run into the bushes. Ben is left with a twisted can and walks back to the rest home. Serling's voiceover reminds us that Sunnyvale rest home is a place for people who have forgotten the "fragile magic" of youth.[3]

This optimistic tale of magic stands in contrast to the usual *Twilight Zone* fare but it shows us that Serling retained some of the idealism of the Binghamton of his youth. The idea that there is nothing of greater value than mind and spirit and that human nature retained a measure of optimism and compassion, as Rousseau said, leads to the idea that democracy as a political society was the best of all possible worlds, as Serling says in "The Mind and the Matter." These are the ideas of Tom Paine and Jefferson, belief in the goodness of mankind and the ability of people to govern themselves based on equality and fairness. Serling shows in these stories that he is in their camp.

The "Trade-Ins" and "The Chaser" are optimistic and deal with the theme of magic. In the "Trade-Ins" an elderly couple, Marie and John Holt, go to the New Life Corp to get new bodies because their old ones (he is 79 and she is 74) are wearing out. They are there to look for new "human receptacles" and the director of New Life takes them to a showroom of models. It's scary, but this is an optimistic tale and the Holts will reject youth to be together. They do not live in the world of "Eye of the Beholder" where looks, and ideas and virtues, are dictated by the state. For Serling, not only don't "differences weaken us" but they make us stronger and that's the greatness of a free society.

Serling says that the Holts are looking for a "magic printing press" but it's too expensive and they can only afford one new receptacle which they agree John can get. John tries to win money at a poker game to purchase a receptacle for Marie, but he does not get the money. So he buys himself a new receptacle and emerges as a young man but when he sees Marie he realizes that he is alone. Good thing they save his old receptacle so he can go back to his old self. They reverse the process and John and Marie walk into the "sunset" to

Serling's voiceover that love triumphs and Khalil Gibran's quote from *The Prophet* that "love is sufficient unto love."

"The Chaser," written by Robert Presnell based on a story by John Collier, shows magic in a different way—too much of a good thing. In this story, doors open by themselves when Roger Shackleforth asks Professor A. Daemon for a love potion for Leila. The professor says that love potions are the "parlor trick" of his profession and they cost one dollar but he keeps making reference to the "glove cleaner" which is $1000. Roger doesn't want glove cleaner, he just wants the love potion.

The love potion works and Leila gives Roger his pipe and slippers to the theme of the *Romeo and Juliet Overture*. But Roger can't take it and he goes back to the professor who charges him $1000 for the "glove cleaner" that reverses the spell. But Roger is too timid to use it so the story illustrates the proverb: be careful what you wish for, it might come true. We see the professor on the terrace of Leila's apartment blowing smoke rings. This story is about magic, but magic only works if you use it and, as with most things in *The Twilight Zone*, it has a flip side.

Magic is also part of "The Whole Truth" where a magic car that makes the owner tell the truth is purchased by Khrushchev, the Soviet leader.

Love potions and glove cleaners aside, there is optimism in a variety of *Twilight Zone* shows including "Nervous Man in a Four Dollar Room" and "Ninety Years without Slumbering" which are both about self-help and the ability of people to remake themselves. "The Fear" has a similarly optimistic message—that even though people are motivated by fear, they can renounce it. The message of "Changing of the Guard" is optimistic—that people can change their thinking and sometimes magic can help.

We see Jackie Rhodes as the "Nervous Man in a Four Dollar Room" in a flophouse hotel room. He is a small time hit man and criminal who answers to a bigger criminal. The bigger criminal controls Jackie by fear. Jackie looks in the mirror, a favorite device also used in "The Mirror," "The Last Night of a Jockey," and "The Big Tall Wish," and talks to himself. He wonders why he became a hood and the Jackie in the mirror tells him he can stop being a hood if he wants to.

When Jackie's boss comes to the hotel room to ask why Jackie didn't do the hit Jackie says he quits and renounces his gun. He looks in the mirror and now the Jackies flip—the nervous and nail biting Jackie is now the man in the mirror wondering "what's to do" and the citizen Jackie is in the room. He calls up the hotel and says the room is too dirty for him—it's a dump. This is a tale of redemption for Jackie Rhodes—the idea that, if you play by the rules, you can change your thinking.

Magic and self-help is also the theme of "Ninety Years without Slumbering,"
written by Richard deRoy based on an unpublished short story by George
Clayton Johnson, where a senior citizen takes his phobia into his own hands
with help from a psychiatrist. Here, an elderly man is paralyzed by fear of his
grandfather clock stopping and conducts his life around that fear. Everything
he does is dictated by the fear—he gets rid of the clock and sells it to his
granddaughter's neighbor. But that doesn't work, and he tries to break into the
neighbor's house to set the clock. His granddaughter takes him to a psychiatrist who helps him with his fear and he is triumphant. Thus, modern science
helps senior citizens to be bold in the face of fear.

The magic comes in this story when he talks to his soul one night and
commands it to go back into his body proclaiming that he's been to a psychiatrist and he knows that the fear is irrational. Now he is free to take care
of his granddaughter and his great grandchildren. In "Static," a bitter man
named Ed Lindsay is whisked back to a simpler place and time with a magic
radio that gives him a "second chance." Ed Lindsay can connect to the past
and a radio station that went out of business—but only he can. Everyone
else just hears static. The static represents the static state of Ed Lindsay,
but the magic radio gives him an escape and maybe a second chance at
romance.

A magic ring helps an actress save a town in the "Ring-a-Ding Girl," written
by Earl Hamner, Jr. Bunny Blake is a Hollywood movie star who is packing
to go on a trip. Her nickname is the "Ring-a-Ding Girl" because she collects
rings and one arrives in the mail from her fans in Howardville, her home
town, just as she is leaving Hollywood to make a movie in Rome. She decides
to visit Howardville because she holds up the ring and sees her sister, Hildy,
telling her to come home.

Bunny goes home to her sister Hildy's house—she shows up in her sun-
glasses and fur coat with the magic "mood ring" for a day *en route* to Rome.
The Founders' Day Picnic, an annual event in Howardville, is that afternoon
but Bunny looks at the ring and sees a local radio announcer who asks her
to come home. She faints. When a doctor makes a house call she asks him to
postpone the picnic and he refuses because Bunny isn't in Hollywood and she
can't ask those favors.

Bunny sees the custodian from high school in the ring and he asks for
Bunny's help. She goes to the high school to see Mr. Gentry and asks him to
unlock the school auditorium so that people can come to her performance
instead of the picnic—he thinks she's a snob, asking for favors, but tells her
the auditorium is open. She tells him not to go to the picnic.

She goes to the television station to tell people to go to the high school
auditorium for the show—she wants them to go to the show rather than the

picnic. She looks at the ring and sees herself in the airplane. There's a big storm—she looks at the ring and sees the airline pilot saying there's rough weather. Her assistant asks her if she's scared and she replies "isn't everyone?" They hear fire engines and Bunny disappeared.

Her plane crashes but the magic ring allowed her to warn people away from the picnic—her plane crashed into the picnic grounds but most of the citizens were at the school auditorium. Bunny was on the plane—how could she be visiting her sister? The ring is left on the floor of Hildy's house, broken.

The "Ring-a-Ding Girl" is optimistic in a variety of ways—the magic ring allows Bunny to warn the people of her hometown about her plane crashing, it shows the contrast of "Hollywood" and "hometown" (Bunny likes her hometown and didn't "go Hollywood")—and she throws her fur coat on the floor and says of Howardville—"it's so good" she wonders why she left. Here, the magic is used to protect people of her hometown rather than for her career, or for material things. She is a movie star who goes back to her hometown and likes it, it's refreshing, it's not Hollywood and glamour. Written by Earl Hamner, Jr. this is the kind of story that would appeal to Serling because Howardville was like Binghamton.

The story "In Praise of Pip" uses magic and also an anti-war message. The scene is Vietnam where they bring in a soldier on a stretcher—he has shrapnel wounds—his name is Pip Phillips.[4] His father, Max, is jolted out of bed feeling his pain. Max is a down and out bookie in a room in a rooming house. This story is a reverse of "The Big Tall Wish" because here the adult makes the wish for his kid.

Max gets a telegram that says Pip is wounded—just then he looks out the window at an amusement park with the calliope music which takes him out of his seedy world. In the background the wailing saxophone's cadenza of woe and the nostalgic and lilting melody of a distant calliope brought to mind happier days but the wailing saxophone and atonal dissonant sounds told a tale of woe. Max wants to go back to when Pip was a child and they went to the amusement park.

The crooks with Max get into a brawl and Max is wounded. He talks to Pip and tells him he's going to reform—meanwhile in Vietnam they're working on Pip. Max wanders into an abandoned amusement park and imagines he sees Pip as a child. The midway lights up and we see the carousel going round in the background. Max and Pip go on all the rides—the music is dissonant to show the fantasy. Now Pip runs into the fun house where everything is a fantasy. Max "wished and hoped instead of tried" and Pip is slipping away—but in reality so is Max from his wound. The funhouse glass shatters and Max is left alone. The lights go out and Max pleads—he makes a wish—he says "Take me, take me."

Max's wish comes true and he collapses. We see Pip in his army uniform and walking with a limp, returned from Vietnam where, according to Max, we shouldn't be at war. This story, "In Praise of Pip," is really in praise of miracles and, as Serling says, the power of magic and love to transcend even war.

"A Passage for Trumpet" also features a theme of magic—this show is like "The Big Tall Wish." Joey Crown is a down and out musician—he says he's nothing. The horn is his language. When he's drunk he pretends he's Gabriel. He sells his trumpet, stumbles out of a bar and is hit by a truck. He walks on the street but no one can see him—he is a ghost. They don't hear him—also symbolic of alienation, and De Tocqueville's idea that "he is close to them, but does not see them; he touches them, but he does not feel them."[5] He thinks it's a joke, but when he looks in the mirror he doesn't see himself. The bartender can't hear him—nobody sees him.

He sees a man playing the trumpet who can see and hear him. Joey plays his trumpet, the man, Gabe, knows his name. Joey is in limbo just like Bolie Jackson in "The Big Tall Wish." The man asks if Joey prefers the "real" world. Now Joey appreciates things, he wants to go back. He has talent.

Joey goes back and sees himself lying on the street, but he gets up (unlike Bolie, the boxer in "The Big Tall Wish"). The driver of the truck gives him money which he uses to buy back his trumpet. Now he's happy—he sits on a rooftop and plays—a lady, Nan, appreciates it and asks Joey to show her the town. Serling agrees with Homer—"better a serf on Earth than a king in the underworld."[6] Joey "Crown" doesn't want to be a king—he wants to be who he was.

Like Joey Crown, Agnes Grep in "Cavender is Coming," doesn't want to be rich in a mansion. Agnes Grep is awkward, but apprentice angel Harmon Cavender is going to try to help her to get his wings. But, Serling tells us, this is a story about miracles. Agnes is fired from her job as an usher at Plotsky's Bijou.

She takes the bus home and Cavender is next to her. He tells her that he's her guardian angel and he can use miracles to help her, so he can get his wings. She doesn't believe him, but he says he'll show her a miracle—instead of riding in the bus he puts them in a convertible with a driver (but he is a bumbling angel and first they are in a horse drawn carriage).

She goes to her apartment and Cavender is there. He is going to make her wealthy so that she doesn't need a job. He gives her money and puts her in the Morgan mansion on Sutton Place. He snaps his fingers and they are at an elegant party at her mansion. He makes the best martini, another miracle.

She tries to go to her apartment but it's been rented—she tells Cavender she wants friends. She doesn't want to go back to the Morgan mansion, she wants to stay at her apartment—but he wants her to be at the mansion so he can get his wings.

Cavender uses his magic and she stays in her apartment. Cavender says that he tried the miracles, but she wanted to go back to where she was. She was happy just being her, like Joey Crown and Mr. Bevis. Cavender says she's rich even though she doesn't have money. Cavender's boss says he can be assigned to more projects because his assignment was to make Agnes happy.

Agnes Grep and Joey Crown need magic to show them that they are really happy and Serling says that sometimes, if you need magic, it's under "M" in *The Twilight Zone.*

Do we need magic for democracy? Do we need the idea that humans are capable of governing and ruling themselves?

Of course Serling was a reluctant Hobbesian, but so were Tom Paine and Jefferson. The Federalists, the founders like James Madison, were optimists—even with a negative view of human nature, as expressed in *The Federalist Papers,* they believed in democracy, the political theory of the optimist who believes that people can be better than their human nature would allow them, often out of self-interest.

In Federalist #55 Madison says there are "qualities in nature which justify a certain portion of esteem and confidence . . . there is a degree of depravity in mankind which requires a certain degree of circumspection and distrust." And famously, in Federalist #51, Madison said "if men were angels, no government would be necessary." Madison says in Federalist #10 "so strong is this propensity of mankind to fall into mutual animosities that where no substantial occasion presents itself the most frivolous and fanciful distinctions have been sufficient to kindle their unfriendly passions and excite their most violent conflicts."

Even though all of these statements seem to say that Madison has a negative view of human nature, nobody would say he was not an optimist in writing the US Constitution and founding a democracy. So even with the negativity, there has to be some "magic" for the founders, as they admit in the *Federalist Papers,* in order to write a document like the Constitution.

According to James Madison, in Federalist #37, this belief is important because, speaking of the American Revolution and the Constitution "It is impossible for the man of pious reflection not to perceive in it a finger of that Almighty hand. . . ."[7] And John Jay in Federalist #2 says "Providence has been pleased to give this one connected country to one united people."[8] So the American founders believed that we need a sense of magic or spirituality to engage in democracy or republican government, just as Serling believed in the power of magic to make people realize their potential.

The Allegory of the Cave

Perhaps there is no more illuminating political image than Plato's "Allegory of the Cave" from *The Republic*. Plato, the Greek philosopher, explains the plight of man, chained in a cave and forced to look at images that flicker across the cave wall. The cave, for Plato, represents ignorance and darkness, as opposed to the "real" world that the former prisoner experiences when he is set free to experience higher knowledge outside the cave. For Plato, everything inside the cave is fake—the images, the appearances are simply shadows of the real world outside the cave. Plato compares knowledge of the Good to the sun.

Marx also comments on the cave: "we have said . . . that man is regressing to the cave dwelling . . . the savage in his cave—a natural element which freely offers itself for his use and protection—feels himself no more a stranger, or rather feels himself to be just as much at home as a fish in water. But the cellar-dwelling of the poor man is a hostile dwelling."[9]

The cave appears in several *Twilight Zone* shows often with a variety of meanings. For Serling the cave image is invoked variously to represent safety (as in "The Old Man in the Cave," "The Rip Van Winkle Caper," "The Shelter" and "A Quality of Mercy") and ignorance as in "On Thursday We Leave for Home."

In "On Thursday" Captain Benteen keeps his captive audience entertained with stories of Earth but everything that occurs on the planet is only a shadow of the real world of Earth. What did the cave symbolize to the inhabitants of the planet? Safety and shelter and a way to escape the suns of the planet, but also ignorance, darkness as opposed to enlightenment. They run into the cave for shelter in the meteor shower. In Platonic theory, the darkness of the cave represents ignorance and the sun enlightenment. So it's no coincidence that when the inhabitants come out of the cave they see two suns and are enlightened and want their freedom.

Plato's discussion of the Line of Cognition brings out the ways in which we are "enlightened or unenlightened" and the most childish level of understanding in the cave, as opposed to the most sophisticated level of understanding that goes on outside the cave, is represented by images that bear little resemblance to reality.[10] The life that is lived completely inside the cave, therefore, is the life of ignorance. The two suns of the planet represent enlightenment and thinking and when the inhabitants come out of the cave to go to Earth they no longer need a leader, no longer need Captain Benteen. They understand the idea of the good which, for Serling, is freedom and individualism as opposed to Captain Benteen's collectivism.

For Plato, the people in the cave don't know they are living in ignorance— because the cave is all they come in contact with so they consider it the real world. But the real world only exists outside of the cave. How, then, does anyone know that reality exists outside the cave? They must be dragged out by those outside the cave, i.e., the rescuers. When the prisoners experience the higher pleasures outside the cave they don't want to go back. As with the people in "On Thursday We Leave for Home" Plato says that the prisoners who leave the cave—here, Captain Benteen's cave—don't want to go back and if the prisoner who leaves the cave "called to mind his fellow prisoners" and what seemed like "wisdom in his former dwelling-place, he would surely think himself happy . . . and be sorry for them."[11]

Colonel Sloane is the equivalent of Platonic Guardians who drag people outside the cave to freedom. Immediately outside the cave the former inhabitants make plans to go to California, Chicago, etc. They will act as individuals not as a group and they reject Benteen's collectivism just as Serling rejected collectivist ideology. The cave is the world of appearances and Benteen's stories are like the images on the wall of Plato's cave.[12] When everyone else leaves the planet Benteen chooses to stay, he chooses the fantasy of the cave over reality and only when he is alone does he realize his folly.

In "The Rip Van Winkle Caper" the cave is used literally to represent a place of safety until the crooks can exit the cave and go out with their gold. Here, four crooks steal gold and scheme to put themselves in a cave only to come out later. The scheme works and they emerge from the cave to the real world—but their gold is worthless because now it can be manufactured. So, again, the cave is a place of safety but also deception and false promises. It is a place where the stories of the state are manufactured, for Plato and Captain Benteen.[13]

Another literal use of the cave is "The Old Man in the Cave" where the cave represents wisdom. In a flip to Plato's cave the old man, who is a computer, is the only wise one in the town demolished by nuclear war. People go into the cave to ask what they can do, such as what they can and cannot eat, and when a policeman comes to challenge the old man in the cave he is wrong and the old man in the cave is right. The only man standing is the one who listened to the old man in the cave.

For both Plato and Serling the cave is a place of safety but also a place of deception. If we think of "The Shelter" and "Time Enough at Last" these basement shelters represent safety from the belligerence of people. In "The Shelter" the shelter is a place of safety for the wise—the ignorant are outside because they didn't build shelters. But though it is a place of safety it is not a place of reality which is only outside the shelter with hate, prejudice, and belligerence.

In "A Quality of Mercy" the cave becomes a hiding place for the Japanese soldiers and represents safety for them, as their American counterparts outside of the cave try to figure out what to do with them. As in "The Shelter," there is wisdom inside the cave and the ignorant are outside discussing war. The American lieutenant wants to go into the cave and kill the Japanese soldiers, but when he turns into a Japanese soldier he sees the other point of view. Now he is not that willing to go in, now he is not so sure that war is the right thing to do. The cave figures prominently in this drama, even though the action takes place outside the cave it comes to represent the world of dreams and shadows compared to the outside world of reality which, as Serling admits, is sometimes worse than a place of illusions.

In "Time Enough at Last" we also see the shelter or cave at Mr. Bemis' bank as a place for the wise—him. The people who are at the bank and everyone else was not in the shelter when the war started but Mr. Bemis, a wise man, was in the shelter reading books so he was safe. But Serling brings up the the question: what is he safe for? Though the cave seems like a safe haven, as in Plato's *Republic* it is a place of deception and false illusions. Perhaps Serling is in agreement with Plato—for Serling, and for Plato, people usually prefer their deceptions and illusions as in "Miniature," and the "Rip Van" "Winkle Caper."

For Serling, the cave is the twilight zone—the shadowy world between darkness and light, with flickering images, where fantasy and reality compete, "between night and sunrise or between sunrise and full night" according to Webster. The cave is limbo, as in "The Big Tall Wish" where Bolie Jackson is in limbo, "A Passage for Trumpet" where Joey Crown is in limbo, "In Praise of Pip" (Max is in limbo), "Long Distance Call" (Billy) and "An Occurrence at Owl Creek Bridge" (the prisoner is in limbo). Some can get out of the cave (Joey and Max in "In Praise of Pip" and "A Passage for Trumpet" and Billy in "Long Distance Call") but Bolie Jackson and the prisoner go back to the cave.

Conclusion

Rod Serling said humanity was his business.[14] He was a writer using science fiction, *The Twilight Zone*, to show human nature and political themes such as fascism, the individual v. the state, war, justice and prejudice. Though many of the shows include violence and humans at war, some shows include the theme of magic and generosity.

Plato told the story about the Ring of Gyges, a ring that makes the wearer invisible. For Plato, the magic ring symbolized that people will "do right only under compulsion." Gyges was a shepherd for the King who stole a ring and went to a shepherd's meeting wearing the ring:

. . . as he was sitting with the others, he happened to turn the bezel of the ring inside his hand. At once he became invisible, and his companions . . . began to speak of him as if he had left them. Then . . . he turned the bezel outwards and became visible again . . . as he turned the bezel inside or out he vanished and reappeared. After this . . . he contrived to be one of the messengers sent to the court. There he seduced the Queen, and with her help murdered the King and seized the throne.[15]

Plato says that if there were two rings, one given to the "just" man and one to the "unjust" the just "would behave no better than the other" and both would do whatever they wanted because "no one, it is commonly believed, would have such iron strength of mind as to stand fast in doing right or keep his hands off other men's goods."[16]

But in "A Penny for Your Thoughts" and "The Prime Mover" characters have "iron strength of mind as to stand fast in doing right" and they do not use their powers as Gyges in Plato's story. Serling says that people will do wrong—but they will also do right.

The show "A Penny for Your Thoughts," written by George Clayton Johnson, uses the same theme as the Ring of Gyges—what would happen if you could read minds? How would you use that information? Would you use it to help other people or yourself? What does this tell us about human nature?

Here, Hector Poole, who is going to work at a bank, pays for a newspaper with a magic coin that stands on its end. The newsboy tells Hector that it must be his lucky day and he's right because the magic coin gave Poole the ability to hear people's thoughts. Poole is a bank clerk, a symbol in *The Twilight Zone* of the alienation and bureaucracy of modernity. This is the impersonal, bureaucratic, work-a-day cog in the wheel job in other *Twilight Zone* shows—like "Mr. Bevis," "The Mind and the Matter," "Time Enough at Last." These employees believe their bosses don't appreciate them and they don't like their jobs.

But can Hector Poole use his magic coin the way Gyges used his magic ring? Does Serling agree with Plato that people do good only under compulsion?

Poole's boss is Mr. Bagby and he can now read his thoughts. He hears that Mr. Bagby is having an affair. This is information that he can use to his advantage so that he can get a better job and more respect at the bank. But, unlike Gyges, he uses his powers to save the bank from someone who would use his loan to bet on horses. Poole hears the thoughts of a worker, Mr. Smithers, who is going to rob the bank and go to Bermuda. He tells Mr. Bagby and Mr. Bagby tells the guard to open Mr. Smithers' briefcase—but there's no money. Smithers did not rob the bank—he only *thought* about robbing the bank. It was just his daydream.

Mr. Smithers asks Poole how he knew that he was thinking of robbing the bank and going to Bermuda. He says that this is a dream of his—another bank clerk in *The Twilight Zone* who daydreams. He wants to rob the bank, but won't. It's his fantasy.

Bagby fires Poole, but gives him his job back when the man to whom the bank gave the loan tries to use bank funds to bet on horses. But Poole wants a better job and threatens to tell Mr. Bagby's wife about his affair. Poole blackmails Mr. Bagby—but he also asks for a round trip ticket to Bermuda for Mr. Smithers! He uses his magic coin for good—not just for himself. He walks Miss Turner home and buys another newspaper from the same stand and knocks over the magic coin—now Poole doesn't have the power to read minds. Poole thinks it's good that he doesn't have the power, because he doesn't want an unfair advantage at work, etc. unlike Gyges.

Poole is happy he doesn't have power to do whatever he wants with impunity—unlike Gyges. According to Plato, human nature of the just or unjust man is the same—people want to do whatever they want with impunity whether with a magic ring or coin. But Serling says that even if Poole used the magic powers to blackmail his boss so he could get a good job at the bank he also used the powers for Smithers—which would not benefit him.

The two sides of Poole's coin are like the happy and sad faces of drama—people won't only do things like murder and steal, like Gyges, they will also buy things for people. Serling agrees with Plato and says that people will do bad, like Gyges and Mr. Poole blackmailing his boss, but Serling says they will also do good and he continues this theme in "The Prime Mover" written by Charles Beaumont based on a story by George Clayton Johnson.

Ace Larsen owns the Happy Daze Café and Jimbo Cobb works there. Jimbo has telekinesis, the power to move things. He moves a car and he moves a bed, he flips a coin and he flips dice. Ace, a gambler who has a one arm bandit at the café, says they're going to Las Vegas to use Jimbo's power to their advantage. Jimbo's talent makes them win, but he gets a headache.

They bring up boxes of money to their hotel room but Jimbo doesn't want to do it anymore—it's unethical. Jimbo is the "just" man and Ace the "unjust" but for Serling they act differently—Jimbo says that Ace's girlfriend, Kitty, is worth more than money. Ace asks him to use his powers one more time to gamble against Phil Nolan, a gangster. The next morning the phone rings and Jimbo levitates it to his bed—it's Mr. Nolan. Nolan comes to the room to gamble and they play with his dice. Ace bets all his money but Jimbo's power wanes and they go home broke.

Back at the Happy Daze Café men take away the one arm bandit. Now Ace asks Kitty to marry him, even though he's broke. Now Jimbo's power comes back—maybe it didn't wane, maybe he just didn't want to use his power the way Gyges used it, maybe people don't always only do right under compulsion, as Plato said. Would Gyges throw away the ring? Plato says no but Serling says yes—he is not completely soured on human nature and people. Both Poole and Jimbo Cobb reject the Gyges advantage.

Perhaps the two most optimistic stories are "The Obsolete Man" and "On Thursday We Leave for Home" in which Serling states his optimism in individualism and democracy, people governing themselves. Serling has always expressed his preference for the individual over collectivist theories but nowhere more eloquently than in these two shows which are optimistic in the sense of the triumph of the individual over collectivism.

Clearly, Serling's belief in democracy was strengthened by his fighting for it against the collectivist ideologies of World War II. When he enlisted in World War II he was enlisting for democracy and even though his belief in people acting together to govern themselves is not always his theme, the theme is represented in these shows in a way that states Serling's view of democracy as the best government because of its belief in the individual.

Aristotle had a theory known as "The One, The Few, and The Many" relating to "right" and "wrong" governments. According to Aristotle, governments can be ruled by a person, a few people, or the many but we must also ask "for what purpose" do they govern—themselves, or for the good of everyone?

According to Aristotle

> the sovereign must necessarily be either One, or Few, or Many. On this basis we may say that when the One, or the Few, or the Many, rule with a view to the common interest, the constitutions under which they do so must necessarily be right constitutions. On the other hand the constitutions directed to the personal interest of the One, or the Few, or the Masses, must necessarily be perversions. (They deviate from the true standard by not regarding the interest of all. . . .)[17]

Serling considers "The One, The Few, and The Many" in such shows as the "Eye of the Beholder," "The Little People," "On Thursday We Leave for Home," "It's a Good Life," "The Obsolete Man."

Serling considers "The One" and dictatorship in the "Eye of the Beholder" where there is one idea, one creed and the "one dictator" is shown on television indoctrinating the people. Here, "the one" is not only one idea or creed but one idea of beauty. Serling rejects this as tyranny and dictatorship. He also rejects the dictatorship of Captain Benteen in "On Thursday We Leave for Home," and the dictatorship of Anthony Fremont (or "Freemont"—nobody is free with dictatorship) in "It's a Good Life," and the dictatorship of Peter Cook in "The Little People." As Aristotle said, dictatorship is where one person rules for his own benefit, rather than the benefit of everyone.

In "The Obsolete Man" the society is ruled by a "board"— "The Few." Here, they decide who is "obsolete" such as the librarian played by Burgess Meredith. The government by "The Few" according to Aristotle is an oligarchy or an aristocracy both of which are rejected by Serling and Aristotle as not democratic enough. Aristotle likes the common man and says "feasts to which many contribute" are better than feasts with one cook. He believes in collective wisdom, and that common people have common sense.

Aristotle, Hobbes and Serling like "the Many" of democracy. For Aristotle, the government is the Polity and for Serling the individual rules in a democracy which he said in "The Mind and the Matter" was the best of all worlds: "with all its faults . . . this is the best of all possible worlds." Serling rejects "The One" and "The Few" but he likes "The Many" of "On Thursday We Leave for Home." Here, the people reject Captain Benteen's collectivism.[18] They want to go back to Earth where they can be free individuals, not ruled by a dictator but with freedom. Serling likes democracy, individualism and freedom, as he says in "The Obsolete Man" "any state, any entity, any ideology that fails to recognize the worth, the dignity, the rights of man, that state is obsolete."

Also, like De Tocqueville, he is against the "Tyranny of the Majority" of conformity. Tocqueville says of the tyranny of the majority "unlimited power is in itself a bad . . . thing . . . human beings are not competent to exercise it with discretion . . . the power of the majority surpasses all the powers with which we are acquainted in Europe" and "raises formidable barriers around the liberty of opinion" and "I know of no country in which there is so little independence of mind and real freedom of discussion as in America" and questions whether "such a jury" ought to control so much power.[19] De Tocqueville thought that the free institutions would be clobbered by the "Tyranny of the Majority" and the trend toward government power.

What would Serling have said about such events as the fall of the Berlin Wall, the election of the first African-American president, and Cuba?

Because Serling rejected collectivism ("The Mirror," "On Thursday We Leave for Home") we can only think that he would be delighted about the fall of the Berlin Wall. "Little Girl Lost," written by Richard Matheson, aired in March 1962 when the Berlin Wall was news—it had been constructed in August 1961. This is a story about Mr. and Mrs. Miller who hear their daughter and go looking for her but they don't see her—she has fallen behind the wall of her bed into another dimension. She's not under the bed—she's in the Twilight Zone.

The dog runs under the bed and also goes behind the wall. The Millers call their neighbor, a physicist, who puts his hand through the wall. Chris Miller puts his hand through the wall and falls into the other dimension. He grabs his daughter and pulls her and the dog through the wall. Now the wall is closed up.

Perhaps Serling would consider society behind the Berlin Wall the Twilight Zone—we know he rejected any government or theory that denies the rights of the individual. Chris pulling his daughter through the wall is like the West pulling the East through the wall—and Serling probably would have applauded that.

What would Serling have said about the election of the first African-American president? He would be delighted at the important step toward racial equality in America and the achievement of a dream rather than "A Dream Deferred" by Langston Hughes. Perhaps he would think that it smacks of the scintillating and heady tone of the clarinet in "Rhapsody in Blue" as it glides up the cadenza to its zenith. This is an American story, and he would take pride in the achievement of a great goal in the march against prejudice and bigotry which he wrote and spoke about in his work and would hail it as a "victory for mankind." In fact, Serling wrote about this, the writing based on a novel called "The Man" by Irving Wallace about an African-American president.

What would Serling have said about Cuba still being communist after the fall of the Soviet Union? Considering his work on dictatorship, such as "The Mirror" which specifically addresses this question he would probably be surprised. How could communism still be in Cuba after the fall of the Soviet Union? This is a mystery, not only to Serling. Perhaps the dictator is not his own enemy, the message of "The Mirror," but perhaps he is his own best friend.

Serling would have been interested in the story of Elian Gonzalez, the Cuban boy who fled Cuba in 2000 and was rescued by a fisherman, Donato Dalrymple. This story combines the elements that Serling could have used for a *Twilight Zone*—an escape from dictatorship, children and magic. The magical part is that Elian clung to an inner tube on his float to Miami where other members of his group perished, was saved by dolphins who kept the sharks at bay and a fisherman who may be remembered as he stood in a closet with Elian as the US government took him back to his father in Cuba at gunpoint.

Like Hobbes, Serling believed that people could work for a democracy—unlike Hobbes, he agreed with De Tocqueville: if we give government enough power to do good, we've also given it enough to abuse people with. His work in "On Thursday We Leave for Home" and "The Obsolete Man," among others, demonstrates his belief in the individual and the individual's ability to rule himself and govern the state and the planet. What would Serling say about 9/11? He would probably say that the worst thing about evil is its terrible accuracy and, as usual, he would be right.

Perhaps most important, Serling would want people to try to rise above their belligerent nature and the alienation of modern society to become a community. As he said at Moorpark College in 1968, quoting Spanish philosopher Uno Mono and reminiscent of "The Midnight Sun": "Men do not die of the darkness . . . they die of the cold. It is the frost that kills. That's what the dream is. That's what it's all about. The oneness of men." With a reference reminiscent of "Time Enough at Last" he said: "I think the destiny of all men is not to sit in the rubble of their own making but to reach out for an ultimate perfection which is to be had. At the moment it is a dream. . . . But we have it within our power to make it a reality." As Abby said in "No Time Like the Past": "I guess that's all that's left sometimes—just hope."

Notes

1. Zicree, Marc Scott, Author's Note on the Second edition to *Twilight Zone Companion.*

2. Plato, *Republic.* Translated by G.M.A. Grube. Revised by C.D.C. Reeve. (Indianapolis: Hackett Publishing Company, Inc., c1992), xii–xiii, p. 100, IV. 424.

3. According to Serling this theme comes from a wish to return to his youth, "Submitted for Your Approval," *American Masters*, PBS TV show.

4. Serling was wounded in World War II.

5. De Tocqueville, *Democracy in America*, Modern Library, Book IV, ch. vi, p. 583.

6. "I would rather be on earth as the hired servant of another, in the house of a landless man . . . than be king" of the underworld, Homer, *The Iliad*, xxiii, quoted in Plato, *The Republic*, p. 76.

7. Madison, *Federalist Papers*, p. 230–231(New American Library, NY, 1961) Intro by Clinton Rossiter.

8. Ibid., Federalist #2, p. 38.

9. Marx, Karl, "Economic and Philosophic Manuscripts of 1844" quoted in *Marx and Engels Reader*, p. 100.

10. Plato, *The Republic*, p. 227 translated by Francis MacDonald Cornford (Oxford University Press, London: 1975).

11. Plato, T*he Republic*, Francis MacDonald Cornford (Oxford University Press, NY:1975) p. 230.

12. Kaytee Lozier who also suggests that in "Miniature" the dollhouse is the cave, a "fake world of illusions" to which Charley escapes.

13. Plato says the cave is where "Noble Lies" are told by the state including the Allegory of the Metals which segregates people based on innate qualities.

14. "Submitted for your approval," *American Masters*, PBS.

15. Plato, *The Republic*, translated by Francis MacDonald Cornford, p. 44–45.

16. Ibid., *The Republic*, p. 45.

17. Aristotle, *The Politics*, translated by Ernest Barker (Oxford University Press, London: 1958) p. 114.

18. Perhaps Serling changed his mind about collectivism because of Vietnam saying "I reject in principle this business of . . . blood-letting simply because the opponent is a Communist" from *LA Times*, June 25, 1967 "Serling in Creative Mainstream" by Ellen Cameron May.

19. De Tocqueville, *Democracy in America*, "The Unlimited Power of the Majority" p. 145–158.

Bibliography

Aristotle. *The Politics*. Translated by Ernest Barker (London: Oxford Univ. Press, 1958).

De Tocqueville, Alexis. *Democracy in America*, with Introduction by Thomas Bender (New York: Modern Library, 1981).

Efron, Edith. "Can a TV Writer Keep His Integrity?" *TV Guide*, April 21, 1962.

Epictetus. *The Art of Living: The Classic Manual on Virtue, Happiness and Effectiveness*. Translation by Sharon Lebell (New York: Harper Collins, 1995).

Hobbes, Thomas. *Leviathan*, ed. CB Macpherson (New York: Penguin Books, 1980).

Hobbes, Thomas. *The Elements of Law* (London: Simpkin, Marshall and Co, 1989).

Kramnick, Isaac. "Equal Opportunity and the Race of Life." *Dissent*, vol. 28, 1981.

Locke, John. *The Second Treatise of Government*, ed. CB Macpherson (Indianapolis: Hackett, 1980).

Madison, Hamilton and Jay. *The Federalist Papers*, with Introduction by Clinton Rossiter (New York: New American Library, 1961).

Marx, Karl. "Economic and Philosophic Manuscripts of 1844" and "The Communist Manifesto" in *Marx and Engels Reader*, ed. Robert C. Tucker (New York: W. W. Norton, 1978).

May, Ellen Cameron. "Serling in Creative Mainstream." *Los Angeles Times*, June 25, 1967, p. C22.

Ollman, Bertell. *Alienation: Marx's Conception of Man in Capitalist Society*, 2nd ed. (New York: Cambridge University Press, 1976).

Paine, Thomas. *Common Sense*, with Introduction by Isaac Kramnick (New York: Penguin, 1986).

Pietaro, John. "Rod Serling: For Your Consideration." *Political Affairs*, www.political affairsnet/article/articleview/7940.

Plato. *The Republic*. Translated by Francis MacDonald Cornford (London: Oxford University Press, 1975).

Plato. *The Republic.* Translated by GMA Grube, revised by CDC Reeve (Indianapolis: Hackett, 1992).

Rousseau, Jean-Jacques. *The Social Contract and Discourses.* Everyman's Library (Great Britain: JM Dent and Sons, 1973).

Sander, Gordon F. *Serling: The Rise and Twilight of Television's Last Angry Man* (New York: Dutton, 1992).

Serling, Rod. Speech at Moorpark College, Los Angeles, December 1968.

Vinciguerra, Thomas. "Marley Is Dead, Killed in a Nuclear War." *New York Times,* Dec 20, 2007, p. E12.

Wagner, Thomas and John Goff. "Submitted for Your Approval." *American Masters,* PBS television show, 1995, produced and directed by Susan Lacy.

Zicree, Marc Scott. *The Twilight Zone Companion,* 2nd ed. (Los Angeles: Silman-James Press, 1989).

Zicree, Marc Scott. Liner notes to CBS VHS Columbia House *The Twilight Zone.* CBS VHS Video, Treasures of the Twilight Zone, interview Oct, 1959.

Twilight Zone Episode Guide

<hr>

Shows Written by Rod Serling

The After Hours (1st season)

The Big Tall Wish (1st season)

The Brain Center at Whipple's (5th season)

Cavender is Coming (3rd season)

The Changing of the Guard (3rd season)

Deaths-Head Revisited (3rd season)

The Dummy (based on an unpublished story by Lee Polk) (3rd season)

Dust (2nd season)

Escape Clause (1st season)

Execution (based on an unpublished story by George Clayton Johnson) (1st season)

The Eye of the Beholder (2nd season)

The Fear (5th season)

The Fever (1st season)

Five Characters in Search of an Exit (based on a short story by Marvin Petal) (3rd season)

Four O'Clock (based on a short story by Price Day) (3rd season)

The Gift (3rd season)

He's Alive (4th season)

The Hitch-Hiker (based on a radio play by Lucille Fletcher) (1st season)

Hocus-Pocus and Frisby (based on an unpublished story by Frederic Louis Fox) (3rd season)

I Am the Night—Color Me Black (5th season)

In Praise of Pip (5th season)

I Shot an Arrow Into the Air (1st season) (based on an idea by Madelon Champion)

It's a Good Life (based on a short story by Jerome Bixby) (3rd season)

The Jeopardy Room (5th season)

The Last Night of a Jockey (5th season)

The Lateness of the Hour (2nd season)

The Little People (3rd season)

The Lonely (1st season)

The Man in the Bottle (2nd season)

The Masks (5th season)

The Midnight Sun (3rd season)

The Mighty Casey (1st season)

The Mind and the Matter (2nd season)

The Mirror (3rd season)

Mirror Image (1st season)

The Monsters Are Due on Maple St. (1st season)

A Most Unusual Camera (2nd season)

Mr. Bevis (1st season)

Mr. Denton on Doomsday (1st season)

Nervous Man in a Four Dollar Room (2nd season)

Night of the Meek (2nd season)

Nightmare as a Child (1st season)

No Time Like the Past (4th season)

The Obsolete Man (2nd season)

Of Late I Think of Cliffordville (based on a short story by Malcolm Jameson) (4th season)

The Old Man in the Cave (based on a story by Henry Slesar) (5th season)

On Thursday We Leave for Home (4th season)

A Passage for Trumpet (1st season)

The Passersby (3rd season)

People Are Alike All Over (based on a short story by Paul Fairman) (1st season)

Probe 7—Over and Out (5th season)

The Purple Testament (1st season)

A Quality of Mercy (based on an idea by Sam Rolfe) (3rd season)

The Rip Van Winkle Caper (2nd season)

The 7th is Made Up of Phantoms (5th season)

The Shelter (3rd season)

A Short Drink from a Certain Fountain (based on an idea by Lou Holtz)
(5th season)

The Silence (2nd season)

The Sixteen-Millimeter Shrine (1st season)

Still Valley (based on a short story by Manly Wade Wellman) (3rd season)

A Stop at Willoughby (1st season)

A Thing about Machines (2nd season)

The Trade-Ins (3rd season)

Third from the Sun (based on a short story by Richard Matheson) (1st
season)

Time Enough at Last (based on a short story by Lynn Venable) (1st season)

To Serve Man (based on a short story by Damon Knight) (3rd season)

Twenty-Two (based on an anecdote in *Famous Ghost Stories*, ed. by Bennett
Cerf) (2nd season)

Uncle Simon (5th season)

Walking Distance (1st season)

What You Need (based on a short story by Lewis Padgett) (1st season)

Where is Everybody? (1st season)

The Whole Truth (2nd season)

Will the Real Martian Please Stand Up (2nd season)

Not Written by Serling

The Bewitchin' Pool by Earl Hamner, Jr. (5th season)

Black Leather Jackets by Earl Hamner, Jr. (5th season)

Caesar and Me by A. T. Strassfield (5th season)

The Chaser by Robert Presnell (based on a short story by John Collier) (1st
season)

Elegy by Charles Beaumont (1st season)

The Encounter by Martin M. Goldsmith (5th season)

From Agnes with Love by Bernard Shoenfeld(5th season)

The Fugitive by Charles Beaumont

The Grave by Montgomery Pittman (3rd season)

The Howling Man by Charles Beaumont (2nd season)

I Dream of Genie by John Furia, Jr. (4th season)

I Sing the Body Electric by Ray Bradbury (3rd season)

The Incredible World of Horace Ford by Reginald Rose (4th season)

In His Image by Charles Beaumont (4th season)

The Invaders by Richard Matheson (2nd season)

The Jungle by Charles Beaumont (3rd season)

Kick the Can by George Clayton Johnson (3rd season)

Little Girl Lost by Richard Matheson

Living Doll by Jerry Sohl, plotted by Charles Beaumont and Jerry Sohl (credited to Beaumont) (5th season)

Long Distance Call by William Idelson and Charles Beaumont

Miniature by Charles Beaumont (4th season)

A Nice Place to Visit by Charles Beaumont (1st season)

Nick of Time by Richard Matheson(2nd season)

Nightmare at 20,000 Feet by Richard Matheson (5th season)

Ninety Years without Slumbering by Richard deRoy (based on a story attributed alternately to Johnson Smith and George Clayton Johnson) (5th season)

Nothing in the Dark by George Clayton Johnson (3rd season)

Number Twelve Looks Just Like You by John Tomerlin, credited to Charles Beaumont (5th season)

An Occurrence at Owl Creek Bridge by Robert Enrico (based on a short story by Ambrose Bierce) (5th season)

Once Upon a Time by Richard Matheson (3rd season)

Perchance to Dream by Charles Beaumont

Person or Persons Unknown by Charles Beaumont (3rd season)

A Piano in the House by Earl Hamner, Jr. (3rd season)

The Prime Mover by Charles Beaumont (based on an unpublished story by George Clayton Johnson)

Queen of the Nile by Jerry Sohl, plotted by Charles Beaumont and Jerry Sohl (credited to Beaumont) (5th season)

The Ring-a-Ding Girl by Earl Hamner, Jr. (5th season)

The Self-Improvement of Salvadore Ross by Jerry McNeely (based on a story by Henry Slesar) (5th season)

Spur of the Moment by Richard Matheson (5th season)

Static by Charles Beaumont (based on an unpublished story by OCee Ritch) (2nd season)

Steel by Richard Matheson (5th season)

Stopover in a Quiet Town by Earl hamner, Jr. (5th season)

Two by Montgomery Pittman (3rd season)

A World of Difference by Richard Matheson (1st season)

A World of His Own by Richard Matheson (1st season)

You Drive by Earl Hamner, Jr. (5th season)

Index

subject theme, 48–49. *See also* state of nature
humanity, contribution to, 1, 4–5, 8, 11, 32–33, 132
Hunnicut, Harvey ("The Whole Truth"), 101–2

"I Sing the Body Electric" (Whitman), 115n2
Idelson, William, 120
ignorance, 130–31
individual, 109; against state, 4, 7, 57–59, 61–63, 75–76, 79, 97

Jackson, Bolie ("The Big Tall Wish"), 67, 103, 119–20, 128, 132
Jagger ("I Am the Night—Color Me Black"), 65–66
Jameson, Malcolm, 53n22
Jay, John, 129
Jefferson, Thomas, 124
Jessica ("In His Image"), 89–90
Jews, prejudice against, 95–96, 103
Jody ("Third from the Sun"), 107–8
Johnson, George Clayton, 23, 24, 123, 126, 133, 134
Johnson, Russell, 64
Johnson administration, 88
justice and the law, 64, 67–72, 80n11; retribution, 28–29, 51, 70–72; war crimes, 71–72, 73, 103

Kanamits ("To Serve Man"), 46–47, 101
Keaton, Buster, 114
Kelly, "Steel" ("Steel"), 88
Kennedy, John F., 7, 77, 98, 99, 100, 102
Kennedy, Robert, 98
Khrushchev, Nikita, 101–2, 125
Knight, Damon, 46
Koch, Sheriff ("Dust"), 121
Kuchenko, Ivan ("The Jeopardy Room"), 100–101

Larsen, Ace ("The Prime Mover"), 134–35
laws, 58–59
Leila ("The Chaser"), 40, 125
Leviathan (Hobbes), 33, 78–79, 83, 85
liars, theme of, 30–31
limbo, 128, 132
Lincoln, Abraham, 95
Lindsay, Ed ("Static"), 126
Line of Cognition, 130
Little Big Horn, 75
Locke, John, 58–59, 68, 71
loneliness, 5, 35, 48–50, 49–50, 54n30, 90, 112–13
lookism, 4
Loren, Jana ("Lateness"), 84
Loren, William ("Lateness"), 84
Lozier, Kaytee, 138n12
Lucas, Curt J. ("Four O'Clock"), 67–68
Luddites, 86, 115n6
Luis ("Dust"), 65
Lutze (Mr. Schmidt) ("Deaths-Head Revisited"), 71–72, 99

Machiavelli, Nicolò, 2, 33, 34, 98
machines: acquisitiveness and, 11–12; anti-mechanism, 85–86; automata, concept of, 3, 33, 37, 83–85; blurring between machines and people, 3, 84–85, 88, 109–10; blurring of people with, 84–85; dummies and dolls, 84, 85, 86, 88, 89; mannequins, 85, 109–10, 113; Marxist view, 87–88; overreliance on, 84–85; pursuit by, 2, 12, 68–69, 70, 80n11; science and, 83–85
Madison, James, 129
Maggie ("One for the Angels"), 31
magic, 8, 119–29. *See also* superstition
Maitland, Leah ("The Self-Improvement of Salvadore Ross"), 38
Mann, Horace, 4, 6, 9n4, 32, 33, 123
"The Man" (Wallace), 137
Marcia ("The After Hours"), 85

About the Author

Leslie Dale Feldman is professor of political science at Hofstra University. She has had visiting fellowships at Princeton University and the University of California at Berkeley sponsored by the National Endowment for the Humanities and is a recipient of the Distinguished Service Award from the New York State Political Science Association. She is the author of *Freedom as Motion* and co-editor of *Honor and Loyalty: Inside the Politics of the George H.W. Bush White House.*

Breinigsville, PA USA
29 September 2010
246291BV00002B/5/P